The Brain

A Comparative Look into the Physical & Spiritual Mechanics of Your Brain

By Nancy A Connell

i

ISBN: 9780997454130

<u>Contact the Author:</u>
shiningyourglory@gmx.com

For more prophetic Words by other prophets and to be fed fresh manna from Heaven to grow deeper in your walk with God, visit: www.lighthousechurchinc.org

Other books by Nancy & Brett Connell:

A Remembrance
ISBN: 9780986157202

Heavens Courts
ISBN: 9780997454109

Exorcism in a Brand New Way
ISBN: 9780997454123

How to Defeat the Enemy of Your Mind
ISBN: 9781548027483

The Spirit of Jealousy
ISBN: 9781979862943

Parenting God's Way
ISBN: 9781533361516

Instructions from the Father Vol.1
ISBN: 9780986157226

Instructions from the Father Vol.2
ISBN: 9781537387994

Instructions from the Father Vol.3
ISBN: 9781981447114

Resources

http://www.innerbody.com/

http://www.strokeeducation.info/brain/

https://en.wikipedia.org/wiki/

http://brainmadesimple.com/

http://webspace.ship.edu/cgboer

http://serendip.brynmawr.edu/bb/kinser/Structure1.html

https://www.youtube.com/

https://www.webmd.com/

Disclaimer

Thank You!

First and foremost I want to thank my Heavenly Father for all the patience He has for Me and the encouragement and strength He has given to help see me through this project.

I would like to thank my one and only Savior Jesus Christ, who does sit on the throne of my heart, and who I am getting to know more and more every day for the love that has been shown to me as this book was coming together, that if it only helps one soul it is so worth it.

I would like to thank my best friend, my guide, my voice of truth, the Holy Spirit for without the Godhead this book would not have been possible.

I would like to thank my husband Brett Connell, for your love, support and encouragement, through the good and bad days, and for helping to put the book together and making sure that everything is in order and correct.

I would like to thank my mentor, my friend, my shepherd, my spiritual parent who always has confidence in me, to encourage me to be obedient to God in all that He asks me to do, Evangelist Barbara Lynch.

I would like to thank my family for being there to take care of one another as this book came together and giving me time to sit before God and allow Him to write the revelations that He wanted in the book.

Thank you for all your hard work and time you have put into it to make it possible, Evangelist Barbara Lynch, Rev. Brett Connell, Rev. Christopher Gore, Rev. Elaine Betts, Duncan and Lynda Connell, Rev. Adam Betz, Rev. Aaron Betz, and for the art work, Jade Focht. I really do appreciate the parts that each of you played in getting this book out for people to glean from and gather information that they may not have known and to bring them into a deeper prayer life with God.

Table of Contents

Preface

In this book you will find that there are many functions and processes going on within the brain that we will address. There will be the explanation on how your brain works in different areas on a beginner's level. It has been through a lot of research from many people and textbooks that these notes and expressed knowledge have been put together. Things are subject to change so please feel free to do your own research and allow the Holy Spirit to show you more in depth things that are going on.

Next you will find different spiritual things being addressed and referenced to. There will be direction and instruction leading to prayer for healing, exorcism, ministry, and inner searching of yourself. We are not speaking of two brains at this point. We are speaking of the brain and just in different realms of it.

This is all focused upon God, the Almighty that the Holy Bible talks about that sits on the throne of Heaven and is the Author and Finisher, the Great Creator, The Great I AM of Heaven and of Earth. It is focused upon His Son Jesus Christ, who died upon the Cross for our sins and then was resurrected and now sits at the right hand of the Father forever interceding for us. It is also focused upon the Holy Spirit that God the Father sent here as a helper, a guide, and a comforter to aid us in this walk with Him as Jesus ascended from this earth to be seated with God. So this is what is made up of the Holy Trinity and that is referred to all throughout this book on the spiritual part.

There are arguments of whether or not a Christian can have a demon, to what is ok and not ok with sexual perversion, and even whether or not women should or should not preach the Word of God. The truth is each answer to this is in the Word of God.

We have been too long fighting each other about the Word of God instead of working together to bring in the sheep to the sheep fold. To bring in the lost and dying souls should be our top priority. We need to be in a position where God can bring them into safety and not into a torture chamber that the Body (of Christ) has started to make it.

Too many people have fallen into the traps of learnt behavior, expecting that the corruption of the mind is acceptable, and that we are stuck being bound instead of realizing that the only thing that was saved was your spirit-man. You have to die to your flesh and rid yourself of the world and become a sacrifice for Christ. As you continue to study on the brain and use the knowledge here to expand your way of thinking and praying, you will see a tremendous change on every aspect of your life.

In this book you will find that there is quite a bit of instruction on how to root out and address demon spirits. Can a Christian have a demon spirit? Yes they can. When you are born again, your spirit-man becomes a brand new creation in Jesus Christ. But your soul is still wounded, bound, and needs to be liberated from the effects of sin and demon spirits. Your soul consists of your mind, your will, and your emotions.

In the Word of God, Jesus would go to the temple and heal the sick, cast out spirits, and minister the Word. When He would walk in the world it was those who came to him and followed him that He would also heal and cast out spirits. Here are a few Scriptures to look upon:

Luke 11:14 (NIV)
Jesus was driving out a demon that was mute. When the demon left, the man who had been mute spoke, and the crowd was amazed.

Matthew 8:16 (NIV)

When evening came, many who were demon-possessed were brought to him, and he drove out the spirits with a word and healed all the sick.

Mark 1:34-39 (NIV)

34 and Jesus healed many who had various diseases. He also drove out many demons, but he would not let the demons speak because they knew who he was.
35 Very early in the morning, while it was still dark, Jesus got up, left the house and went off to a solitary place, where he prayed.
36 Simon and his companions went to look for him,
37 and when they found him, they exclaimed: "Everyone is looking for you!"
38 Jesus replied, "Let us go somewhere else—to the nearby villages—so I can preach there also. That is why I have come."
39 So he traveled throughout Galilee, preaching in their synagogues and driving out demons.

Matthew 12:9-15 (NIV)

9 Going on from that place, he went into their synagogue,
10 and a man with a shriveled hand was there. Looking for a reason to bring charges against Jesus, they asked him, "Is it lawful to heal on the Sabbath?"
11 He said to them, "If any of you has a sheep and it falls into a pit on the Sabbath, will you not take hold of it and lift it out?
12 How much more valuable is a person than a sheep! Therefore it is lawful to do good on the Sabbath."
13 Then he said to the man, "Stretch out your hand." So he stretched it out and it was completely restored, just as sound as the other.
14 But the Pharisees went out and plotted how they might kill Jesus.
15 Aware of this, Jesus withdrew from that place. A large crowd followed him, and he healed all who were ill.

Matthew 12:22 (NIV)
Then they brought him a demon-possessed man who was blind and mute, and Jesus healed him, so that he could both talk and see.

Mark 9:25 (NIV)
When Jesus saw that a crowd was running to the scene, he rebuked the impure spirit. "You deaf and mute spirit," he said, "I command you, come out of him and never enter him again."

Your soul did not get messed up overnight so be patient as this process continues over the course of your lifespan; as you are working on getting it perfected and cleansed so that God can use you without any defilement of His temple (you). Know that when you are casting out these demon spirits that you are to be filling yourselves with the Holy Spirit and that you are staying in the Word, getting a relationship with God and keeping your spirit-man filled and clean. There is a danger of casting out spirits but not following through with your walk with God and getting right.

Matthew 12:43-45 (NIV)
43 "When an impure spirit comes out of a person, it goes through arid places seeking rest and does not find it.
44 Then it says, 'I will return to the house I left.' When it arrives, it finds the house unoccupied, swept clean and put in order.
45 Then it goes and takes with it seven other spirits more wicked than itself, and they go in and live there. And the final condition of that person is worse than the first. That is how it will be with this wicked generation."

So please, as you are going through this book, always allow the Holy Spirit to lead, guide, and direct you. Minister in the name of Jesus Christ and do what we have been commissioned to do and that is:

Matthew 28:16-20 (NIV)
16 *Then the eleven disciples went to Galilee, to the mountain where Jesus had told them to go.*
17 *When they saw him, they worshiped him; but some doubted.*
18 *Then Jesus came to them and said, "All authority in heaven and on earth has been given to me.*
19 *Therefore go and make disciples of all nations, baptizing them in the name of the Father and of the Son and of the Holy Spirit,*
20 *and teaching them to obey everything I have commanded you. And surely I am with you always, to the very end of the age."*

John 14:12-14 (NIV)
12 *Very truly I tell you, whoever believes in me will do the works I have been doing, and they will do even greater things than these, because I am going to the Father.*
13 *And I will do whatever you ask in my name, so that the Father may be glorified in the Son.*
14 *You may ask me for anything in my name, and I will do it.*

And do the works that Jesus did:

Matthew 10:7-8 (NIV)
7 *As you go, proclaim this message: 'The kingdom of heaven has come near.'*
8 *Heal the sick, raise the dead, cleanse those who have leprosy, drive out demons. Freely you have received; freely give.*

Mark 16:15-20 (NIV)
15 *He said to them, "Go into all the world and preach the gospel to all creation.*
16 *Whoever believes and is baptized will be saved, but whoever does not believe will be condemned.*

17 And these signs will accompany those who believe: In my name they will drive out demons; they will speak in new tongues;

18 they will pick up snakes with their hands; and when they drink deadly poison, it will not hurt them at all; they will place their hands on sick people, and they will get well."

19 After the Lord Jesus had spoken to them, he was taken up into heaven and he sat at the right hand of God.

20 Then the disciples went out and preached everywhere, and the Lord worked with them and confirmed his word by the signs that accompanied it.

Acts 5:12-16 (NIV)

12 The apostles performed many signs and wonders among the people. And all the believers used to meet together in Solomon's Colonnade.

13 No one else dared join them, even though they were highly regarded by the people.

14 Nevertheless, more and more men and women believed in the Lord and were added to their number.

15 As a result, people brought the sick into the streets and laid them on beds and mats so that at least Peter's shadow might fall on some of them as he passed by.

16 Crowds gathered also from the towns around Jerusalem, bringing their sick and those tormented by impure spirits, and all of them were healed.

Introduction

Through this book, by the leading of the Holy Spirit, it is my desire that you will come to a greater understanding of how your brain functions in the natural and in the spiritual realm. I pray that you will gain spiritual knowledge and healing that will lead to the freedom and transformation that God desires for you.

Ephesians 1:17-21 (NIV)
17 I keep asking that the God of our Lord Jesus Christ, the glorious Father, may give you the Spirit of wisdom and revelation, so that you may know him better.
18 I pray that the eyes of your heart may be enlightened in order that you may know the hope to which he has called you, the riches of his glorious inheritance in his holy people,
19 and his incomparably great power for us who believe. That power is the same as the mighty strength
20 he exerted when he raised Christ from the dead and seated him at his right hand in the heavenly realms,
21 far above all rule and authority, power and dominion, and every name that is invoked, not only in the present age but also in the one to come.

One of the major problems we are suffering from is a lack of knowledge. We do not understand how God has created our mind to function. God has equipped us with His Word to be able to become transformed. This transformation will cause us to truly become like Christ and live holy as He has said to do.

1 Peter 1:15-16 (NIV)
15 But just as he who called you is holy, so be holy in all you do;
16 for it is written: "Be holy, because I am holy."

Our mind consists of our flesh. We have to crucify the flesh so that we can walk in the Spirit. This means we need to have a change of lifestyle, a change in our belief system, as well as an understanding of how to walk continuously in this change.

Galatians 5:16 (NIV)
So I say, walk by the Spirit, and you will not gratify the desires of the flesh.

In this book, we are going to take a look at the brain and how it functions. This will teach a new perspective on how to pray for different things that are going on in your life that is affected by what your brain is responsible for or has a part to play in. It will show new prayer strategies for yourself and others to align your thought patterns with the Word of God. Examining the brain will teach you how to destroy old mindsets, reveal different places that demonic spirits can hide, and change how you pray for healing.

This book will not only open your eyes to the various ways in which your brain behaves and affects your bodily functions, but also how those functions of the brain affect you spiritually. When you apply what you learn, you will be able to walk in a newfound freedom that God had intended you to walk in all along.

As you understand the brain and how it works, you will see how the physical elements of your brain are related to spiritual ones. Treating your brain for physical problems is not the same as treating it spiritually. Only dealing with the problem that is physically wrong with your brain while ignoring the spiritual, will train your brain to receive just the physical healing. In order to be whole, the healing must be both physical and spiritual.

A problem continues to exist and persist because the entire problem is not being addressed. Understanding that the problem is a process, and seeing it to the end of that process, you will be able to see and receive the full results. By doing this, you remove the power and faith in the problem, and place the real faith into the power of the problem solver – God.

God has always been a finisher. We can hold onto this. He never starts something that He will not finish or be willing to finish. The truth is, the only thing that stops the process is for us to give up on overcoming the problem.

Philippians 1:6 (NIV)
being confident of this, that he who began a good work in you will carry it on to completion until the day of Christ Jesus.

When God created us, He did so with fine detail to be fully functional. I pray that throughout this book, God will give you great wisdom and revelation on how to have your mind transformed into the mind of Christ. I pray you will receive new tactics on how to pray for others, how to see problems from another perspective that will help people receive healings, and to see new avenues on how to destroy the enemy who has attacked you in areas that you may have never taken into consideration before.

When you read this book, please understand that you can pray this for anyone, but it is most effective for yourself. The reason for this is because of the belief system. Once you begin to pour belief into your mind through your faith in Jesus to help you, it secures the process.

What Do You Believe?

God desires to do wonderful things in your life including using you to do things here on this earth. He wants you to be blessed and not cursed. He wants you to be used to change lives and do the things that His Son did here on earth and even greater things. What is stopping you from receiving and doing these things?

John 14:12-14 (NIV)
12 Very truly I tell you, whoever believes in me will do the works I have been doing, and they will do even greater things than these, because I am going to the Father.
13 And I will do whatever you ask in my name, so that the Father may be glorified in the Son.
14 You may ask me for anything in my name, and I will do it.

One answer to this question is TRUSTING Him and BELIEVING in Him and truly LOVING Him. The enemy knows that if he can place even one seed of doubt in our mind to cause us to question God in some way, then he has successfully destroyed part of our connection with God.

John 10:10 (NIV)
The thief comes only to steal and kill and destroy; I have come that they may have life, and have it to the full.

Questioning God becomes a distraction, a side road. It opens the doorway to doubt, unbelief, and then it continues to roll on from there and can give you a false perception of God. If your mind is messed up and cannot think properly, it can become very difficult to believe, trust, and even love God. When you are full of doubt and unbelief, you can feel like you are in prison with no hope to be released. Your mind becomes programmed to what the enemy wants you to believe, conditioning you to think the opposite of what God intended. The enemy will use the world to do this conditioning by using the ways of trend, society, and that which is acceptable by the status quo.

It is a good idea to learn in basic terms how the human brain works, so that you may understand what is going on and how it mirrors what is taking place in the spiritual realm.

Why does something as easy as believing seem to be so hard to do? So much negativity takes place in our lives each and every day. We are exposed to negativity in our jobs, in our homes, even in the grocery store. It is around us continuously but it really is up to us whether or not we keep it or get rid of it. It is up to us which program we want to live by. Will it be God's, or the world's program?

Many people forget to flush out that negativity. The negativity gets pushed down in our minds, in our heart, and deep into the core of our soul. It ends up becoming a part of us. You may even find yourself at a place where you wonder, "How did I get here?" You may also be asking yourself if you are losing your mind. These questions can be answered, and can change your life from doubt-based to faith-based mindsets and help you to have a healthy mind spiritually and physically.

When you find yourself full of negativity you feel unclean, and surrounded by prison bars. A restriction seems to take place over you due to the junk that has been dumped onto and into us. We forget to empty the dumping grounds. The dumping grounds is the place where we mentally store people's problems that are spoken to us when we lend an ear to be a sounding board when the person has a problem.

The dumping grounds can occur when people come to you relaying their problems as you minister to them, or even as you serve them on the job, in the home, or even in church. The dumping grounds can also take place when you are just being a friend and allowing your friend to vent. If you are not emptying the dumping ground, it piles up. It can cause extremely heavy weights and burdens that God never intended you to bear. To empty these dumping grounds, you need to make sure that you are letting go of the problems by releasing them to God, and letting Him take care of it and not trying to do it yourself. It is important that every day you flush this negativity off of you completely. Let's take a moment and do that right now.

Father:
I am asking you right now to go down into every part of my soul, my body, my heart, my mind, and my spirit that has collected negative things that have been placed on me and in me by life, by people, by myself, and by the enemy.

I ask you to flush every part of me out with your Living Waters and cleanse me. I ask you to release me of the bondage that this negativity has placed me in and bring complete freedom in these areas in the name of Jesus.

Please remove every part of negativity and its effects out of my character, personality, my conscious, subconscious, and any place in my brain, stomach, and heart that it has attached to.

I thank you Father that you have removed these things from me and are helping me to continue to stay cleansed of all negativity, and away from those things that are not good for me to think upon. I ask this in Jesus name. Amen.

You should do a flushing of all negativity daily so you do not accumulate any residue which will cause you to go into bondage all over again. Negativity has so many bad effects upon a person. That is why in the Scriptures God has said:

Philippians 4:8 (NIV)
Finally, brothers and sisters, whatever is true, whatever is noble, whatever is right, whatever is pure, whatever is

lovely, whatever is admirable—if anything is excellent or praiseworthy—think about such things.

As you dig into this Scripture, you will become spiritually cleansed. It is my prayer throughout this book that you will be able to grab many treasures and nuggets from heaven. May it continue to bring you healing and draw you closer to God, so you are able to keep moving forward in all He has called you to do.

As this transformation takes place you will discover that the weight of your problems and negative feelings will no longer weigh down your soul. It is important to flush out your thoughts that are not lined up with the Word of God. When your thought life is lined up with God's Word, you then bare the light and easy burden within your soul.

When negativity begins to take root in your mind and you speak words such as "I can't do this, it is too hard," "I can't make them change," and "I can't do what God expects me to do." The negativity tries to make you believe that these statements are true. If a person believes these temporary bouts of negative thoughts and feelings, the lies of the enemy will take deeper roots into the belief system of the person. Let me remind you that in your own strength these things are impossible. However if your belief and trust is in God, with Him ALL things are possible.

Matthew 19:25-26 (NIV)
25 When the disciples heard this, they were greatly astonished and asked, "Who then can be saved?"
26 Jesus looked at them and said, "With man this is impossible, but with God all things are possible."

Many people do not fully understand the meaning and process of working out of their salvation, and how their lifestyles need to change. Too many times people use excuses of why they cannot carry out what God has instructed them to do. They do not want to do the work that is necessary to live that full life in Him.

Not understanding how your body functions can cause a person not to discern all that is happening to them. Knowledge on how our bodies function can help us to recognize and address spirits that could very well be making us sick, bound up, and blinded to the enemy.

Philippians 2:12 (NIV)
Therefore, my dear friends, as you have always obeyed—not only in my presence, but now much more in my absence—continue to work out your salvation with fear and trembling,

There are a lot of discussions to whether or not a Christian can have a demon. The short answer to this is: Yes. When we become born again, the Holy Spirit fills us within our spirit-man and instantly perfects this aspect of our being. The Spirit of God now dwells within us and we are sanctified – restored back to God and into fellowship with Him through our spirit-man.

However, our soul (which is our mind, will, and emotions) are not instantly perfected nor sanctified. If it were so, then we would not have a sinful or negative thought, desire or emotion. This principle applies to our physical body as well – if it were so, we would not have any blemish nor physical illness. Therefore the body and soul are subject to a lifetime process of deliverance, healing and sanctification – the end fruits of which are perfected when Christ returns and gives us our new Heavenly bodies in the resurrection.

We did not suffer every trauma and negative circumstance in our lives overnight – many wounds and different layers of bondage will take time to heal, to be unearthed, to be processed and actively worked upon to bring about the fullness of healing and restoration.

Throughout the book there are going to be many areas in your brain that will be pointed out of where these spirits can hide, hijack, and control and how to get them out.

The Brain

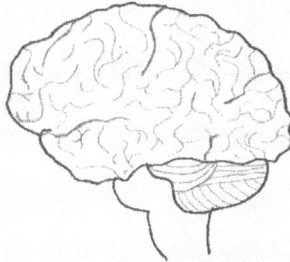

We are going to look at the physical part of the brain and how it is connected to the spiritual part of you. This is just scratching the surface of what has been revealed. Please allow God to show you more revelation. Allow God to take you to a deeper depth of understanding and knowledge in Him.

The brain is one of the most interesting and complicated things to learn about and understand. It is small but it does so many things, and all areas of the body rely on it in order to function properly. It helps you to move, to remember, and help you to be the unique individual that God has called you to be. It is much like the spiritual realm. It is complex and we will forever be learning about it.

There are many avenues to the brain and we are going to touch on a few. Do not put God in a box. Allow Him to show you more as you take this small journey through this book on the brain and seeing the spiritual and physical side of things.

The brain's functions and parts will be broken down; first in the physical, and then it will be broken down spiritually. I pray that this will expand your knowledge, bring you closer to God, and receive any and all healing that you need.

Physically:

The brain is known as the command center of the body. It receives information from the five senses (touch, smell, sight, hearing, and taste) and controls your thoughts, memory, speech, and movements. The brain allows you to think, walk, talk, learn, make friends, have emotions, and be functional to live a productive life.

The brain controls many of these actions through nerve impulses and nerve messages. Bodily functions that the brain modulates can at times take hours or days to register. This is something to take into consideration when you get hurt and the consequences or results do not show up until the next day or so. For example, a bruise usually doesn't become apparent immediately. You may have gotten injured, but the bruise didn't show up until later on in the day or the next day. It is the physical manifestation of the issue reflecting the earlier trauma.

Spiritually:

Keep in mind when you are doing deliverances, exorcisms, and praying for healing, to be patient as things take effect. Results may take time. The requests and healings can be a process. You have to keep moving forward. Be supportive of those areas that have been corrected. Give space to bring forth positive change and freedom.

The average person is believed to have around 70,000 thoughts a day. Excessive thinking has been linked to stress, depression, and paranoia. If you take eight weeks to change your focus from the negative of the world to the positive of God, the result will be sharper memory, increased energy, a longer attention span, and a higher tolerance of pain. Can you imagine the results of what God could really do with this change in thinking? This kind of transformation can make it very uncomfortable for any demonic spirits that may be lodged inside of your brain, as well as any other part of you.

The brain holds a lot of power and contains many functions and systems that affect so many things. Studying the brain is just like studying the spiritual realm. It is a constant learning process because there are so many details and aspects to it. There are so many places for the enemy to hide. This book will help you to root them out and to maintain your freedom.

As you dig into the Word of God it becomes clearer why you need to keep your mind upon Jesus Christ. Clarity will also show you that you must continuously renew your mind. This process allows your mind to be transformed by the watering of the Word of God.

We must pray and give God back the control over our brains and line them up to God's Will and God's Word.

It is also wise to ask God to flush out any thoughts that are not of Him. Pray that every seed of doubt and unbelief that the enemy has placed in your mind will not grow in Jesus' name. Thoughts that are not of God can become footholds that the enemy uses to place you into deception and captivity. These footholds can cause you years of grief. Once you allow the Word of God to be continuously fed into your brain you will see that the washing of the Word brings transformation and destroys what the enemy has been trying to build in you.

Physically:

The brain is continuously changing. The scientific word for this is called neuroplasticity. The more you make positive choices the more often your brain will change its pathways in order to accommodate positive thinking. Repeatedly practicing new habits, behaviors, and thought patterns creates changes in your life to make them more permanent. This is similar to walking down a new path through the woods. The more you walk the same path, the more noticeable that pathway becomes. If you stop walking it, the path will become overgrown with weeds, and hidden by the naked eye.

Spiritually:

In the spiritual realm the brain is one of the things that controls what you allow into your soul. It is a gateway to the heart from the outside to the inside. This is why it is so important to understand how the brain works and processes things, so that you can do your part to control what you are permitting to enter your vessel.

Proverbs 4:23 (NIV)
Above all else, guard your heart, for everything you do flows from it.

When you do this you will also have more confidence in doing what God has equipped and required you to do. You will see and understand the importance of your thoughts, your focus, and what you allow to have access to you. You will understand how it affects your health and the functioning of your body. All of this is done through the mind.

The brain is also one of the biggest targets the enemy goes for and it is on this battlefield that he tries to defeat us. This is where most bondage and captivity takes place. God told us in His Word that we need to take captive every thought into the obedience of Christ.

2 Corinthians 10:5 (NIV)
We demolish arguments and every pretension that sets itself up against the knowledge of God, and we take captive every thought to make it obedient to Christ.

The brain is the command center and it makes perfect sense that the enemy would want to highjack it. He wants to control us. There are many places for him to hide and try to manipulate and deceive us. He wants us to believe that he is invincible but the truth is, he has already lost.

1 John 3:8 (NIV)
The one who does what is sinful is of the devil, because the devil has been sinning from the beginning. The reason the Son of God appeared was to destroy the devil's work.

Colossians 2:15 (NIV)
And having disarmed the powers and authorities, he made a public spectacle of them, triumphing over them by the cross.

You will discover the tools in this book that can be used to destroy the footholds that Satan may have right now. He needs to be challenged and told to leave in Jesus' name. Remember that everything that happens is a process. Jesus took forty days to fast and pray in order to show us that we must persist through all temptations of the enemy. Jesus knew how to come against the enemy with the Word of God. Can we do no less?

Matthew 4:1-11 (NIV)
1 Then Jesus was led by the Spirit into the wilderness to be tempted by the devil.
2 After fasting forty days and forty nights, he was hungry.
3 The tempter came to him and said, "If you are the Son of God, tell these stones to become bread."
4 Jesus answered, "It is written: 'Man shall not live on bread alone, but on every word that comes from the mouth of God.'"
5 Then the devil took him to the holy city and had him stand on the highest point of the temple.
6 "If you are the Son of God," he said, "throw yourself down. For it is written: "'He will command his angels concerning you, and they will lift you up in their hands, so that you will not strike your foot against a stone.'"

7 Jesus answered him, "It is also written: 'Do not put the Lord your God to the test.'"
8 Again, the devil took him to a very high mountain and showed him all the kingdoms of the world and their splendor.
9 "All this I will give you," he said, "if you will bow down and worship me."
10 Jesus said to him, "Away from me, Satan! For it is written: 'Worship the Lord your God, and serve him only.'"
11 Then the devil left him, and angels came and attended him.

Notice how the devil took the Word of God, the strategy that Jesus was using against him, and tried to turn it around, but Jesus did not stop. He kept pressing forward with the Word of God and defeated the devil in this battle.

It is going to take perseverance and practice in order for this transformation to take place and for your mind to become like the mind of Jesus. You have to be very careful on what you are putting into your mind and meditating on. In order to see the patterns change you must do your part consistently until it becomes a part of your lifestyle. Pay attention to the books, internet, music, movies, and things on social media that you watch, read, or sing. Would you do it or look at if Jesus was right there with you?

What you allow your mind to stay focused on will determine how quickly you are healed. If you are continuously thinking about what someone has done to you, then that wound cannot be healed; but will continuously bleed in the spirit realm. But if you choose to forgive and apply the Word of God to the wound, the pain will no longer be able to control you or cause you to respond in a way that would not be honoring God.

Mark 2:8-12 (ERV)

8 Jesus knew immediately what these teachers of the law were thinking. So he said to them, "Why do you have these questions in your minds?
9-10 The Son of Man has power on earth to forgive sins. But how can I prove this to you? Maybe you are thinking it was easy for me to say to the crippled man, 'Your sins are forgiven.' There's no proof it really happened. But what if I say to the man, 'Stand up. Take your mat and walk'? Then you will be able to see if I really have this power or not." So Jesus said to the paralyzed man,
11 "I tell you, stand up. Take your mat and go home."
12 Immediately the paralyzed man stood up. He picked up his mat and walked out of the room. Everyone could see him. They were amazed and praised God. They said, "This is the most amazing thing we have ever seen!"

Food for thought:

Forty days is almost six weeks. This is very close to the eight weeks that scientists say it takes to transform the mind in any area. Think about the awesome things that happen when you spend that much time in God's presence. Think what God can do for your life and the lives of those around you. You may even want to write in a journal what this would look like. Be as specific as possible. Then read and declare it every day.

Challenge yourself, and see where you could make more room for God in your life. This will help your brain. Do you spend time on the phone, texting, playing games, on Facebook, or Twitter? Do you spend time watching sports, exercising, watching TV, etc. that is not integrated with God? If God is separate from your activities of daily living, there is a disconnect that needs restoration.

It really is simple. If you are exercising and improving your body, listening to praise and worship music while working out, or even a sermon to feed your spirit man... putting down the phone and picking up the Word, or speaking to God and praying as you are cooking dinner – you are connecting yourself with God during your busy day and God just loves it when we spend time with Him. Too many people make it a difficult endeavor to spend time with God. It is actually quite easy.

It is time to put religion away and see that God wants a relationship. He is not saying quit living life. He is just asking you to bring Him with you in it. There really is time for God if you are honest. God doesn't ask us to do something that sets us up for failure.

The truth is, we do not want to let go of the flesh. We become selfish and self-centered. We feel a sense of entitlement and these are the things that need to be reprogramed within the brain. The enemy would tell us that serving God is boring or unsatisfactory; but the truth is that our flesh keeps us from enjoying a vibrant and joyful relationship with our Heavenly Father.

We have been programed for so long to be 'all about me' that we do not see how full of self we really are. The brain can indeed be reprogrammed. The mindset is that we assume these habits are 'just our personalities' but these too can be shifted and changed as well.

2 Corinthians 5:17 (NIV)
Therefore, if anyone is in Christ, the new creation has come: The old has gone, the new is here!

Let's now dig deeper and discover more of what occurs in the brain and how to get the brain in the functioning order God has called it. We will then have a greater understanding of what is occurring in our bodies.

The Brain - Reflection and Application:

On average there are about 70,000 thoughts that go through your command center, the brain. Think about what types of thoughts go through your mind. Take a moment and list what you think about the most.

How do you feel that they affect your life, health, and emotions?

Spiritually, how do these thoughts open doors for the enemy to have a foothold in your life?

A course of action on how to get out of these destructive thoughts both physically and spiritually is to read and apply the Word of God to your life and meditate on God. Use the Word of God in your prayer life and stop the enemy in his tracks. Look at your list of thoughts and seek the Scriptures you can use to reverse any negative thoughts that you have and use them against the enemy.

Remember the brain is a road into your heart. So as you are reflecting on your thoughts and cleansing your mind, you are also cleansing your heart and bringing healing to your soul.

Cerebrum – Cortex – Alzheimer Disease

The brain is broken down to three major physical parts.
These are:
- Cerebrum
- Cerebellum
- Medulla (The Brain Stem)

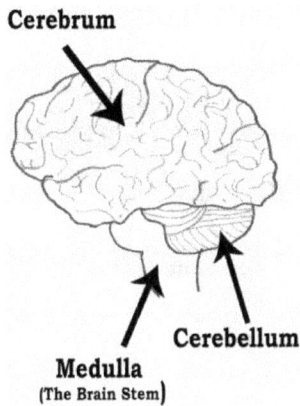

The brain also has four major regions. The four regions are:
- Frontal Lobe
- Temporal Lobe
- Parietal Lobe
- Occipital Lobe

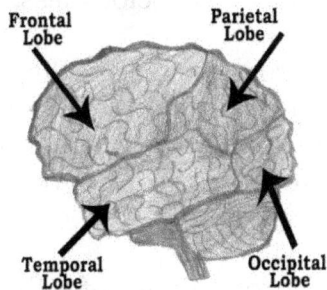

In the chapters ahead, there will be a breakdown of these areas and explanations on how they work. We are going to look at their functions, and how to use this information in prayer, and how to integrate the information into deliverance ministry. The information can also be used in other areas of your life. You will see what may be going on in the physical and spiritual world that is hindering you in your walk with God as well as your daily living in the fullness of health and freedom.

Cerebrum – Cortex

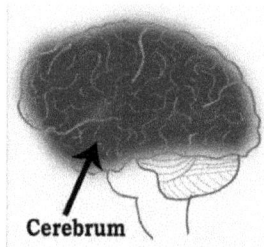

Cerebrum

Physically:

The cerebrum is a large part of the brain. The cerebrum controls your consciousness and your voluntary muscles. It is here that things such as perception, imagination, thought, judgment, and decision occur.

The cerebrum has an outer layer called a cerebral cortex. It consists of folds and wiggly grooves. The cerebral cortex plays an important role in consciousness.

The cerebral cortex provides most of the functions of the cerebrum. It is organized into three regions: sensory, association, and motor areas. The cerebral cortex has to work together as a team in order to control the body and help assure the correct responses.

The cerebrum consists of millions of cells and fibers which send messages to other parts of your brain. It is responsible for processing information from the five senses. It is also responsible for higher thought processing which includes speech and decision making.

The function of the cerebrum is to control your senses, take in the information from your sight, hearing, touch, and other senses; and then interpret the information received. In other words, it would receive, process, and pass the interpretations on to the appropriate areas of the body. Some of these areas have to do with memory, planning and evaluation. It serves as the bridge of information between the senses and how it integrates into thoughts, imaginations, and other parts of the conscious mind.

This is where all conscious thought begins which can influence the subconscious functions of the lower part of the brain. The cerebrum assists the imaginations and thoughts with things like planning, thinking, judging, organizing speech and information.

The cerebrum also controls the execution of muscle movements and is also responsible for generating appropriate responses within the body when external stimulus is processed. For example, if a baseball was hurdling towards us, the cerebrum would fire off signals to the muscles in our arms to lift up and protect our body at the perceived point of impact.

Spiritually:

The cerebrum would be a place to focus on for prayer if you were having issues with things such as not being able to organize your thoughts, being disconnected from your five senses or not functioning correctly, and possibly having the inability to respond correctly in movements.

Looking at it in a spiritual way, you can see that this would be where the entryway to your subconscious would be – as far as communication is concerned. You are going to want to make sure you keep that entryway clean and clear so that any thought, habit or spirit doesn't leak or gain access to your subconscious.

The cerebrum is where you would ask God to cleanse your conscious mind and to clean the path to the subconscious which accesses the lower parts of the brain so you can keep this area of communication clear and functional.

The cerebrum is also where you focus on cleaning your mind of thoughts and imaginations that are not of God. This would be the place where your imaginations could get the best of you and place you into a fantasy world. People with many unhealed heart wounds can develop and 'live in' a fantasy world to 'forget' the emotional pain they felt. It could also be a fantasy world sexually, or even socially. You would want ask God to bring the Truth and remove all alternate realities.

The cerebrum would also be a place where a spirit of deception can reside and give off deceived projections for the afflicted person to believe. It would be the place where you would ask God to remove the lies of the enemy that he projects into your mind in thought form.

Ask God to remove all thoughts and ideas that is not of God so that you are able to concentrate and hold onto what God is doing with you spiritually.

In prayer you can ask God to help you have a filter in this area that would help you to fight thoughts and feelings that the enemy places into your mind. Ask God to remove all vain imaginations that try to exalt themselves over God and command them to come into the obedience of Christ.

2 Corinthians 10:5 (NIV)
We demolish arguments and every pretension that sets itself up against the knowledge of God, and we take captive every thought to make it obedient to Christ.

If God leads, you may also ask the angels to stand watch and guard this part of your brain. This would be the perfect defense, so that the enemy cannot hide and penetrate your mind with the thoughts that alter your perceptions.

The angels also aid the ability to reject things that are not of God. You can ask God to shine His Glory light inside this part of the brain to remove any darkness. Ask God to reveal any hidden thing in there that would try to hijack your thoughts or try to play with your imagination or 'vision'.

Have you ever really paid attention to how many times God says in His Word to keep the focus on Him? Yet for some reason it seems most people only focus on God once they have hit rock bottom. We live in a very self-centered culture where 'It's all about us.'

Proverbs 4:23 (NIV)
Above all else, guard your heart, for everything you do flows from it.

The crazy thing is that even though they were not focusing on God and His words, many people blame God for the situations they are in. So many things would be different in our lives if we would just do it right the first time.

When you are ministering deliverances and exorcisms this is the area that you would remove the images and the lies of the enemy that have been placed inside. You will also address this area with minds that have been living in a fantasy world, and bring them into emotional healing where they can face and understand reality.

Deception and manipulation takes place in this area to deeply root themselves in a person's belief system. When you are doing self-deliverance or if you are going to have deliverance ministry, the spirits to address here are deception and manipulation as you proceed to remove them. This is followed by asking the Holy Spirit to bring to light anything else that is going on in this area so that it can be addressed during this time.

This is an opportunity to pray for the removal of deception from the five physical senses, and full restoration of the perception of the world around them. One could ask God for permission to have the angels of God navigate in these areas and search out where the enemy has infiltrated. You can ask the angels to fix what the enemy has done and to normalize the correct functioning of the senses.

This is the area of the brain that you would want to speak life to where you not only feel cut off in any part of your senses in the spiritual realm, but also in the physical. If you have an illness that specifically is targeted by the functions of the cerebrum you are going to want to uproot the illness and speak regular functions into the malfunctioning areas.

You can focus on this area and ask God to restore your understanding to His understanding so that you are able to take in the wisdom and knowledge that He has downloaded inside of you. A person will want to ask God to seal the truth and remove all lies with the information they have gathered with this part of their brain.

James 1:5 (NIV)
If any of you lacks wisdom, you should ask God, who gives generously to all without finding fault, and it will be given to you.

The cortex part of the brain is where spiritually we are to cast down thoughts not of God. It would also be where we would ask God to remove all information that is not lined up to

God's knowledge and anything that would cause our senses to malfunction.

If you are having issues making decisions, you could ask God to go into your cortex and align it. It would almost be like doing a tune up on your car, but on your brain. You should ask and believe for God to align your thoughts that are being processed. One can also ask the Father to show you what He is doing and how to maintain His cleansing.

If you are having a hard time making a choice you may want to ask God to help cleanse your cortex. Cleansing the cortex will allow you to see, hear, and feel God correctly, so that you can have a clear vision of what is going on. At this point your vision will be cleansed and no longer tainted from what others and the enemy has lodged into this area.

Remember these suggestions are only the beginning on what you can pray for in these areas. Allow God to show you more and address the functioning of that particular part of the brain. Remove any spirits that God tells you to address. Here is an example of a prayer you may pray for yourself and/or others.

Heavenly Father, I ask you to touch my cerebrum and my cerebral cortex and all its functions. I am asking you to cleanse my conscious thought life. I ask you to repair any malfunctions that I have with my senses. I am also asking you Father to line up my voluntary muscles so they work properly.

God, as you are doing this for the physical, I am asking that you mirror the same work in the spiritual. Remove all unclean things from me.

Holy Spirit, please show me where these spirits are in the cerebrum and how to remove them and every root of them. Remove every lie and deception of the enemy and all manipulation. Reveal to me what lies the enemy has planted by shining the truth. Plant the truth in these areas so that I can apply the new changes in my life and be set free.

(You may also address anything that you have been diagnosed with that could potentially affect this region of the brain.)

Thank you, Father, for making me whole and to have a sound mind. Thank you for bringing discipline to the functioning of this area as well as my thoughts. Thank you for cleansing my gates to the subconscious and guarding it with your Angelic Hosts. Thank you for assigning them to protect my subconscious from anything that would try to sneak its way in there from my thought life and catch me off guard.

I speak healing into my cerebrum, freedom into my cerebrum, and balance into my cerebrum. I speak wholeness and correct function to every part of it. And any spirit that is not of God has to be removed and cast straight to the pit in the name of Jesus and everything underneath and all that they brought in with them, every device, tool, weapon, trigger, and assignment removed with them in the name of Jesus.

Father God, I am asking you to help me refocus upon You, Your Will, and Your love that you have called me to live by. Remove my understanding and replace it with Your understanding. Seal it with the truth as each lie is removed in the name of Jesus.

Reconnect me, God, with You and Your presence and love, as my perceptions are lined up with the truth. May true holiness become a part of my thinking patterns and behaviors at all times. I ask of this in Jesus' name Amen

Alzheimer Disease

Let's look at the sicknesses that could be caused by this area malfunctioning and being infested with spirits. Alzheimer

24

Disease is a disease that primarily affects the cortex. So if you know someone with Alzheimer Disease or someone who is starting to show signs, you will want to ask God to reveal to you anything you need to know.

Ask God to show you what is going on in the cortex that needs to be straightened out. When you are asking God to show you this, do so believing that this disease has to go no matter what the medical prognosis is.

Isaiah 53:1 (NIV)
Who has believed our message and to whom has the arm of the Lord been revealed?

Pray and ask God to reverse the damage and claim the healing. Don't give up if it does not happen right away. Keep pressing in and claiming the healing. Ask God to show you the spirits that have taken up lodging and need to be evicted. Start thanking God in advance of the manifestation of healing. This is not a 'religious ritual.'

Psalm 22:3 (KJV)
But thou art holy, O thou that inhabitest the praises of Israel.

Pray and ask God to reverse the report of the enemy and ask the angels to speak God's Will upon their lives. Pray to restore this area of the brain as well as memory and other functions of the brain. This will help remove any roots that have been placed, giving permission for the Alzheimer Disease to be there.

There are some things that come from the generational line. I would encourage you to really look into the depths of this. It may bring you many answers to getting your healing. You may find it is in the genetics or it could be a curse.

If you find out that it is from your generational line or a curse you must break the curses and the generational curses, removing all DNA ties to the Alzheimer Disease. Seek God's face and really be open to what God tells you to pray. This will aid in dislodging this illness from the person. Each case will be unique. This is why it is important to have direct communication with the Father as well as paying very close attention to what the Holy Spirit is leading you to do.

Cerebrum – Cortex – Alzheimer Disease – Reflection and Application:

The three major parts of the brain are: Cerebrum, Cerebellum and Medulla (The Brain Stem). The four major regions of the brain are these four lobes: frontal, temporal, parietal, and occipital.

What is going on in the body in the physical can be a reflection on what is going on in the spiritual body. To receive complete healing, both areas need to be examined and checked out. You can use what you already know to take care of yourself on a personal level with knowledge and wisdom you have attained thus far in life, but when you need outside assistance for more complicated problems you go to a licensed healthcare provider. For spiritual assistance you go to your pastor and/or a deliverance team.

The cerebrum controls things such as your consciousness and voluntary muscles. This is where your perception, imagination, thoughts, judgment and decisions take place. The cerebrum also controls your senses, collects the information that they are taking in, and then interprets the information received.

Spiritually this is the area that you would pray for God to cleanse your conscious mind and to go down the path to the subconscious mind and clean it as well. You can apply the Scripture of taking every thought captive into obedience to Christ and remove all ungodly thoughts and imaginations. As you do this you will be able to see, hear, and feel God correctly and unhindered.

2 Corinthians 10:5 (NIV)
We demolish arguments and every pretension that sets itself up against the knowledge of God, and we take captive every thought to make it obedient to Christ.

27

Pay very close attention to your thoughts. Do they uplift and bring encouragement or do they tear down and destroy with discouragement and no hope?

List some things that go through your mind that causes you to be concerned with the status of your thought life.

Throughout the day examine what is going on in your head and how it affects your daily tasks and your response to others.

Now take a look at your list. Use this list to pray against all the things that do not line up to the Word of God. Take time to find Scriptures to be able to counterattack these thoughts until the entire root is demolished and removed.

Place the influence of your cerebrum back into the hands of God. Ask Him to bring both the physical and spiritual function of your mind to be aligned and function to how He has created you and to line up your reality with the truth so that your physical and spiritual body can function in proper health.

Here is an outline of some questions to get answers to so that you can properly pray over someone who has Alzheimer Disease since it is a disease that primarily affects the cortex in the cerebrum:

1. What symptoms have manifested themselves?

2. What medical diagnosis has been given?

3. Ask God what is damaged and needs to be straightened out? Write down what He says and bring it before Him in prayer.

4. Request that God reverses the damage and claim the healing. Find Scriptures to back up what you are claiming and this destroys any hold the enemy could have.

5. Ask God to reveal what spirits are behind the symptoms of the Alzheimer's and if there is any generational connection. Then rebuke and remove

these spirits by the authority of Christ and cut the generational curses, sin, and anything else that God reveals about this.

Remember each person can be different since we all have different backgrounds, experiences, traumas and a unique makeup in how God made us. So each person you pray for can be different, but the questions above are designed to help you get those different answers.

The Two Hemispheres

Two Hemispheres

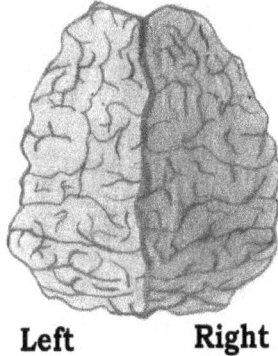

Left   Right

Physically:

The cerebrum is made up of two hemispheres, the right hemisphere and the left hemisphere. If you are right handed then your left hemisphere is the dominant one. If you are left handed your right side of the brain is dominant. Both the left and the right hemispheres are connected by the corpus callosum. Each hemisphere has different functions in the body.

The left hemisphere of the brain is responsible for control of the right side of the body. It is the more academic, logical side of the brain such as being used in science and mathematics. The right hemisphere of your brain is responsible for control of the left side of the body, and is the more artistic, creative side of the brain.

The left hemisphere of the brain is where the language formation is located. It collects the information from the right side of the brain in the forms of pictures or creativity and puts a language skill to it. For example: the right side of the brain would see a visual or picture of a church. The left side would say, "Yes that is a church. It is The Lighthouse Church, where Evangelist Barbara Lynch is the Pastor."

Lesions to this hemisphere will result in a deficiency of language comprehension and speech disorders. Because the left side deals with more of the language and helping to analyze information received into the brain, you would be aware that things are not working properly. You would be unable to solve complicated problems or activities. You can find that people who have damaged the left side of their brain are more depressed than others, have more organizational problems, as well as language issues.

The right hemisphere is responsible for the emotional aspect of language. This side gives you the ability to understand and express language, in the region where the temporal lobe is located. If there are lesions in these areas, the ability to comprehend language will not be affected. It will not contribute to speech disorders either.

Damage to the right hemisphere can result in the inability to emotionalize speech. Someone with damage to this part of the brain would attempt to rationalize humor. This person would not be equipped to diagnose the playful intensions of sarcasm. Such a person may take everything that is spoken literally, and find it difficult or be unable to 'read between the lines' in conversation.

The person who has lesions on their right hemisphere could only comprehend the spoken words and not incorporate the emotions with it. This would result in not being able to understand the playful motive, relying only on literal comprehension, when humor is an abstract thing. Some of these symptoms are similar to what is found in those diagnosed with Asperger's autism.

If one has an injury to the right side of the brain, they could have problems with failing to process important information and experiencing a reduced capacity to mentally piece things together, so to speak. They develop what you could call a denial syndrome and believe wholeheartedly that there is nothing wrong with them. They would have a hard time to realize that something was missing, simply because they were unable to process the information.

Spiritually:

It is helpful to understand the functions of both hemispheres of the brain so that as you experience different issues pertaining to each hemisphere, you will know how to effectively pray in those situations. If for example someone experiences a language problem you can ask God to touch the left hemisphere of the brain to correct it. Perhaps you may know of someone who does not have an emotional attachment to their speech or what they are trying to communicate. In these cases sometimes the person may laugh inappropriately or have what seems like a hard-wired denial system; in these cases you may ask God to touch the right hemisphere of the brain.

If a person is cut off from happiness or is easily offended from what others may take as funny, you can seek God's face and ask Him what is blocking the right hemisphere of the brain. You can speak life and laughter into that person's right hemisphere and destroy the walls and barriers within that hemisphere.

God has a wonderful sense of humor but if someone is blocked in this area, they may not be able to experience it. If you come across someone that is "humbugged" it very well could be that they are blocked and unable to enjoy the emotion of joy, having fun, and enjoying life. They could be blocked off from positive emotions.

Prayers for the left hemisphere of the brain would be geared towards collecting the correct information and putting it together to give clarity, so that confusion and misunderstanding does not settle in. If a person is unable to speak correctly, or has a hard time comprehending, you will want to focus in this area.

This is a place where if someone is having problems in let's say math, you would pray that God strengthens this side of their brain. It would also help to pray for healing this area if you are praying for someone who has issues with complicated problems and shuts down, speech delays and disorders, as well as someone who is disorganized and depressed.

Entering into this kind of thinking on what is really going on with the brain and where in the brain, as well as what is being affected, could very well bring a new revelation on how to get back your joy. This thinking can help remove "stinking thinking," as some would say.

There is so much still to be learned but you can see that this will get the gears of your brain going and help you enter into a deeper prayer life with a different perspective on what you are dealing with.

The Two Hemispheres - Reflection and Application:

Right Side of Cerebrum	Left Side of Cerebrum
Left handed	Right Handed
More artistic and creative	More academic and logical
Understand and express language (emotions behind the words)	Language formation
When damaged:	**When damaged:**
Emotions blocked in words (lack of humor)	Unable to solve complicated problems/activities
Cannot process more than what is directly told	More depressed than others
Becomes "see it to believe it" due to lack of understanding	Organizational issues
Unable to express themselves correctly	Language issues

Do you know someone who is unable to see a problem that is right in front of them? Do you know someone who has a deficiency of language comprehension and speech disorders? You will want to pray for them concerning their left side of the cerebrum.

Do you know someone who is easily offended and has a hard time seeing the humor in others? Do you know someone who has a problem understanding emotions or being able to express their feelings? You will want to pray for them concerning the right side of the cerebrum.

Remember God is all-knowing and all-seeing. God also has a great sense of humor (after all He made each and every one of us.) God wants us to be joyful, enjoy living, being full of life and givers of love. If someone is having a hard time expressing themselves either through words or emotions and being able to process them, it could bring on afflictions of depression, suicide, anger and rage just to name a few. Keep this in mind when you are dealing with spirits as well. Finding out where they are lodged can be a key point in getting someone or yourself completely free.

Lobes

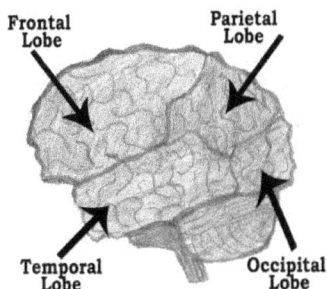

Physically:

The lobes in your brain are separated into the four regions. You have the frontal, parietal, occipital, and temporal lobes. Each lobe is not separated by one another through bones or any other barrier. Each lobe is constantly interacting with one another to process and combine information.

All of the lobes are connected in some way or another. You will also find that each lobe crosses into the right and left hemisphere. They are an integral part of the functioning of the brain and their functions need to be understood. When you have knowledge of this, you will be able to see many parallels to the Spirit realm, and why these areas would become targeted by the enemy.

Spiritually:

There are many things that these lobes do and many areas where the enemy can gain entrance to really wreak havoc in a person's life. It is no wonder there are times that we have deliverances done. There are still places where the enemy will hide if we do not do our part in changing our thought patterns and our lifestyles.

Romans 12:2 (NIV)
Do not conform to the pattern of this world, but be transformed by the renewing of your mind. Then you will be able to test and approve what God's will is—his good, pleasing and perfect will.

The body is made up of trillions of cells. There is always so much going on in those cells at one time. This is where we have to believe and trust that God does a thorough and perfect job. You need to have a belief system to believe for Him to complete the works He starts.

Philippians 1:6 (NIV)
being confident of this, that he who began a good work in you will carry it on to completion until the day of Christ Jesus.

If we would just fully open ourselves to the Holy Spirit, He will reveal to us any hiding place of the enemy. The Holy Spirit would also direct us in what specifically to pray when there is an issue or problem with the body.

As we learn and study about the basics of the brain and how it works, it gives us a foundation for the Holy Spirit to expand on. You will see as you continue to read how the Holy Spirit is intricately involved in the functioning of our bodies. It will build upon the authority of Christ inside of you that you already have.

Psalm 139:13 (NIV)
For you created my inmost being; you knit me together in my mother's womb.

Lobes – Reflection and Application:

All lobes are connected in one way or another and are found in both the left and the right hemispheres of the cerebrum. In the spiritual sense these lobes are entry ways that the enemy uses to gain access to your brain and tries to wreak havoc in your life.

The body is made up of trillions of cells. This is why it is important to consult God, Jesus and the Holy Spirit on what is going on within our brain and how to handle it. They understand the connections and communication that goes on between the lobes and any loop holes the enemy may try to use.

Take a moment and ask God to bring forth the Holy Spirit and teach you how to listen carefully on what healings need to take place and what demonic homes needs to be torn down.

Frontal Lobe

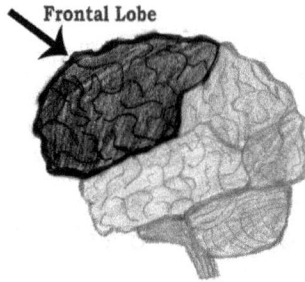

Frontal Lobe

Physically:

The frontal lobes contain the connections to your emotions, personality, and concentration. The frontal lobe also contains connections to the processes of higher thinking and problem solving skills, planning, motivation, and also emotional and social judgments. This is just to name a few.

The frontal lobe is responsible for coordinating complex movements such as playing the piano and for the signals to go to the muscles for voluntary movement.

The frontal lobe also deals with different aspects of behavior, personality, and mood. It regulates the behavior and decision making. A person uses their frontal lobe just about every day. The frontal lobe enables a person to make decisions on what to eat or drink at meal times, helps them think or study for the next lesson, or the test that is going to come up. It also includes the ability to plan.

The frontal lobe is also where the personality develops. It includes the ability to speak smoothly with charisma, feeling, and emotions. The frontal lobe helps manage emotional impulses in socially appropriate ways for productive behaviors including empathy, selflessness, and interpretation of facial expressions.

The frontal lobe also has a place called the Broca's Area. The Broca's area is vital for the information of speech and speech control.

It has been said that the frontal lobe continues to develop until their mid-twenties. This could very well be the reason why it is harder to teach an older person with a fixed mindset.

The frontal lobe helps to regulate the reward and motivation mechanisms; this is why dopamine is released into the brain. Dopamine is a chemical that brings the feelings of reward, pleasure, attention, planning, and memory. If there is damage to the manner in which dopamine is released as well as the amount released, it can cause difficulty with planning, symptoms of ADHD, and symptoms of some memory loss.

When a person has damage to their frontal lobe, they could experience one or more of these symptoms: loss of simple movement of various body parts such as paralysis, inability to plan a sequence of complex movements needed to complete multi-stepped tasks, and loss of spontaneity in interacting with others.

Other signs of damage to the frontal lobe may include loss of flexibility in thinking; persistence of a single thought; inability to focus on the task at hand, mood changes, changes in social behavior, changes in personality, difficulty with problem solving, or inability to express language.

The frontal lobe controls impulses. If a person has damage in this area they may experience difficulty with addiction, aggressive behavior, or other socially inappropriate behaviors.

Some other issues that may show up that would indicate a person may have damage in the frontal lobes are: short term memory loss, interference with long term memory, increased and decreased interest in sexual behavior, and inability to categorize objects. The right lobe damage can also cause persistent talking, run on speech, or perseveration, and increased aggressive behavior.

Spiritually:

This is a place where the enemy can make his plans and where he has one of his strategy rooms. This is where mind control would be able to root itself and cause the most damage. Mind control is anything that would overtake a person's ability to think and reason. For example Satan uses anger, anxiety, fear, etc. as great breeding grounds for his evil doings.

If you would take a look at the evidence of damage to the frontal lobe you will see that there are signs which might indicate spirits of paralysis and crippling; spirits of misunderstanding, spirits of unworthiness; spirits of all the focusing disorders, as well as the spirits that would try to block someone's focus off of God.

There is reason to believe that this would be the place where your mind would get split off into different parts and disassociate. This is where a person has developed a fragmentation that will need to be ministered to and also where someone may have developed schizophrenia. It is where the enemy strikes a person's identity and causes damages to your identity, and causing a person to be in captivity to their past self.

This would be the place to ask God to repair your personality, behavior, and things of this nature. This is where He would remove any foreign parts that have lodged itself within. This area would be were you would focus on praying for emotions to be taken out of captivity and pray for balance and return to normal function as God intended it.

This is the area that God has shown us in many exorcisms that perception of self and of other things become twisted and ruins the belief system. It becomes a part of the person, until deliverance occurs.

When you find yourself having a hard time concentrating or thinking, ask God to cleanse and restore and improve your frontal lobe functions. As you allow Him to do the healing, you will be more in tuned to the Holy Spirit and not what has been your past experiences or behaviors.

There is so much to adjust in this area. It is very important to allow the Holy Spirit the room to show you how to pray for this area and what is involved. This is where true change can take place and where a person can become completely transformed in emotions, character, personality, and even in their everyday living.

2 Corinthians 5:17 (NIV)
Therefore, if anyone is in Christ, the new creation has come: The old has gone, the new is here!

Frontal Lobe – Reflection and Application:

The frontal lobe deals with different aspects of the behavior, personality, mood and decision making. It is believed that the frontal lobe continues to develop until the person becomes the age of the mid-twenties.

When a frontal lobe becomes damaged you may notice different symptoms such as loss in flexible thinking, inability to focus, mood swings, change in social behavior and inability to express in communication to list a few.

Because of all that the frontal lobe does it becomes an easy place for the enemy to lodge a spirit of mind control into this area with the intent to do the most damage. The thinking and reasoning ability can be overridden due to this spirit being there and you could see things such as anger, anxiety, fear and emotions of these come up and interfere with sound reasoning which hinders their ability to make better choices.

When you are faced with a mind control spirit, you may encounter someone with multiple personality disorders, identity issues, perhaps held captive in their past with attachments of spirits of that paralyze and cripples a person in different ways and can also have attachments of spirits of misunderstanding, unworthiness and groupings of focus-related disorders as well as blocking spirits from focusing on God.

Take a moment and reflect if there have been areas in your life where these kinds of things have manifested themselves. Think about and reflect on what was going on and what triggered the reaction. Write down what the root feelings were.

Ask God to remove the poison and take out the taproot of damaged emotions and place inside of you the fruits of the

Spirit and allow those emotions and responses to multiply in abundance.

Galatians 5:22-23 (NIV)
22 But the fruit of the Spirit is love, joy, peace, forbearance, kindness, goodness, faithfulness,
23 gentleness and self-control. Against such things there is no law.

Dismantle the mind control spirit and send it straight to the pit. Attach all those that are working with it and under it. Then ask the Holy Spirit to heal all the wounds and place the influence back into God hands.

Think about different things in your life that you have a hard time letting go of control, and where you think your opinion is necessary. This takes ammo out of the enemy's hands and places the entire situation back into God's hands.

Temporal Lobe:

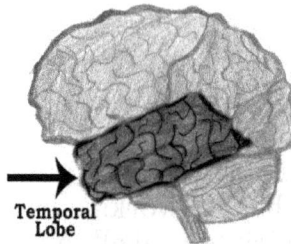

Temporal
Lobe

Physically:

The temporal lobe contains the connections to receive sound from the ears and is the system accountable for the hearing. It is responsible for processing the auditory data from the ears. Auditory data occurs by receiving sensory information such as sounds, volume, pitches, and speech.

It helps make sense of the sounds being transmitted from the sensory receptors of the ears. Sounds and melodies can be recognized. Within the temporal lobe language and reading are linked to being able to comprehend, and these are associated with learning and memory.

The hippocampus which is part of the limbic system is associated with this part. It is responsible for processing long term memory and emotional responses. It assists with the storage of long term memories, and is responsible for the memories associated with the location of objects or people, along with facial recognition.

It is like a memory indexer that sends memories to different parts of the brain and retrieves them when needed. A person has a problem being able to remember where their house was without the work of the hippocampus. This is the area where Alzheimer's disease arises when this area is affected or damaged.

NOTE: There is another part of the hippocampus called the amygdala. When ministering healing to the temporal lobe, healing to the limbic system, hippocampus; the amygdala needs to be taken into consideration.

There are other symptoms of damage to the temporal lobe. Let's take a look at what may demonstrate a person may have issues with their temporal lobe: Things to look for are; difficulty in recognizing faces, difficulty in understanding spoken words, disturbance with selective attention to what is seen and heard, and difficulty with identification of, and verbalization about objects.

Spiritually:

When a person is spiritually looking at the different symptoms and they identify that there is one or more of the symptoms present, they should look into identifying that there is a problem in that lobe. It is best to use those symptoms to pray health and wholeness in that area. Fear should not be a factor. Fear will open the door to more problems. When a person takes the symptoms and prays about it, they will start to see the symptoms be removed as the healing takes place.

This is where the spirit of confusion would easily try to lodge itself. The temporal lobe would be an easy target to make it hard to recognize problems and issues. When a person does not see things in reality it could make it very difficult not to be able to walk in clarity because the spirit of confusion is in operation.

The temporal lobe would be a place where rejection and questioning of the person's self-image would enter. This would also be the place where the enemy would be whispering and planting lies and associating your emotions and connections to different sounds, sights, and tastes.

This is where songs and music would make their impressions. The songs and music would cause a person to find comfort or discomfort in the way the sounds connect to the emotions. A person would be able to put melodies and harmonies together with the words to make songs and worship would form as it makes a connection to them. When that person finds a hindrance in the ability to connect, the enemy very well could have caused a barrier in this part of the brain that would need to be broken down.

The temporal lobe is also the place where the enemy would remove wisdom and information that the person was holding onto, and affect the ability to learn and retain what they are taught. Many times we hear how people are unable to recollect and memorize like they used to while reading the Word of God. A portion of this is due to the influence the temporal lobe has on short and long term memory.

They would also express having such a hard time comprehending. When the enemy places spirits in this area these are a few of the manifestations of it. This is where the enemy can disassociate things from your long term memory and can cause quite a ruckus. But as the enemy is dislodged and removed and healing takes place, these things should begin to become balanced and restored. We have had numerous reports on how much God has done work and opened these areas and have brought a much deeper connection between them and God.

This is also where the deaf spirit both physically and spiritually would try to hide. Often times the enemy has built up things to stop or hinder your ability to hear God as well as those around you. This would be a place where the enemy would cause a communication problem because of a distortion in hearing accurately.

There are many times that we feel that we are being misunderstood; yet in some cases we are not. We have to acknowledge this perspective that we ourselves may be the ones that have the 'tunnel vision' or 'swimmers ear' in the spirit realm. This is when things we are taking in through our senses are muffled or dimmed because of pre-existing issues within us. There have been many times that we heard people discuss their difficulty in hearing and seeing God's plan in their lives even though they are truly serving Him.

They have been diligently seeking God and praying against this hindrance but not getting to the root of the problem; and that could be something has developed, been lodged, been built, or is hiding in the temporal lobe. This is why we are told that there are times we pray and pray amiss. We end up trusting ourselves and not trusting in God and digging deeper to the real root of the problem.

Cleansing the temporal lobe will bring a healing and will clear your ability to hear, and hear properly. You will find many people that will say, "Thus saith the Lord," but will actually have their lobes closed and not understand why things didn't go as planned. They blame everything else rather than looking at the fact that they did not hear correctly. This denial can keep a person in bondage. The reason a person cannot admit to these things is a clear sign there are more spirits in connection with it, and it would be wise to find a place where you can receive deliverance.

So much comes through the temporal lobe and gets collected. This is where your belief system can become hijacked if what comes in does not get dismissed. It would be a very good idea to have the temporal lobe cleansed each night before you go to bed, because even if you were not intentionally listening to things, your subconscious takes in those conversations around you, as well as music, and other things that you are not even aware of. These things can, and do affect you.

Temporal Lobe – Reflection and Application:

The temporal lobe is the connection of the system of hearing of sounds in the ears and working with the hippocampus in processing long term memory and emotional responses. When the temporal lobe is damaged it then becomes responsible for the loss of memory and where Alzheimer's disease arises.

Pay attention to the symptoms of the difficulty recognizing faces, understanding spoken words or selective attention to what the person is seeing or hearing, and difficulty identifying and verbalizing about objects.

If these things are taking place often it would be an excellent idea to go get checked out and then use the doctor's report to pray deeper and follow through with the doctor's orders as you are waiting out your healing.

Spiritually, you need to reflect on whether or not you or the person you are praying for suffers from rejection and questioning their self-image. If so, write down the thoughts or pieces of things that they have said that brings you to this observation; also search and take notice to any whispers of the enemy that has been panted that associates themselves to your emotions and is triggered by different sounds, sights, and tastes. Write them down and go back in memory on when these took place the first time and work on the roots of them.

How is your reception to the sounds of songs and music, especially during praise and worship time with God? List the songs that bring meaning to your heart.

Ask God to remove any hindrance to music and sound that brings Him joy and has been blocked inside of you and anything that would block you from entering into true praise and worship.

If you find yourself having problems hearing, address the deaf spirit and cast it out, remove any fluid that may be causing you to have a swimmer's ear. These issues may require you to look for deeper deliverance and reaching out to a deliverance team so that you know everything is being heard and that the spirit is not trying to deceive you and leave a part of it behind.

Important advice is to cleanse your temporal lobe daily. You can simply ask God to cleanse your temporal lobe each night before you go to bed. Remove all things that your subconscious picked up during the day. Remove all ungodly music, conversation, television, and anything that went undetected when out in the world doing regular daily things.

Think about and list what different things you may think you are picking up on as you are out grocery shopping, watching your children play sports, or simply taking out the trash. What are your ears picking up on?

Wernicke's area

Physically:

The back part of the temporal lobe is the usual location of the Wernicke's area. The function of the Wernicke's area is to help interpret and comprehend spoken and written language. It is connected to the Broca's Area with nerve fibers that allow them to work together to understand language.

If this area of the brain is damaged due to disease or trauma it becomes as some researchers would call, aphasia. Aphasia is described as the loss of ability to understand or express speech, caused by brain damage.

Aphasia can be a result of a stroke, but it can also be found as a result from infections, tumors, and head trauma. When this area is damaged language aphasia can also be a result.

Spiritually:

The Wernicke's area is where the spirits of scrambling, misunderstanding, misinterpretation, deception, and etc. can lodge themselves causing physical damage to your temporal lobe to destroy your connection and trust with God.

When your body goes through a traumatic event to the head, physically or emotionally, you can see how your language could be affected. Think about instances when you may have gotten confused and not been able to communicate what you needed to. Think back and see the times you may have been overwhelmed and felt traumatized and unable to speak or comprehend what others were saying.

It would be something to look into to see that this would be a great breeding ground for a leviathan spirit to lodge itself; or any spirit that would try to cause you to not understand the Word of God while the Pastor is preaching.

If you have had a person who has suffered from a stroke, disease, infections or trauma to their Wernicke's area, then it would be advisable to ask the Holy Spirit to help you pray for that person's wholeness and be able to have the cause reversed.

Isaiah 53:4-5 (NIV)
4 Surely he took up our pain and bore our suffering, yet we considered him punished by God, stricken by him, and afflicted.
5 But he was pierced for our transgressions, he was crushed for our iniquities; the punishment that brought us peace was on him, and by his wounds we are healed.

It is time to see that we need to speak life into these areas and take back our entire vessel and not leave one area untouched.

Wernicke's area – Reflection and Application:

The Wernicke's area is to help interpret and comprehend spoken and written language. If damage or trauma happens to this part of your brain you lose the ability to understand or express speech. They call this Aphasia.

This is where spirits known as the scrambler, misunderstanding, misinterpretation, deception and like spirits can lodge themselves and cause physical manifestations as well as spiritual manifestations.

Have you had a hard time finding words to communicate, or understanding the words expressed by others, that you just don't get what they are saying?

List how you felt during those times and ask God to reveal any spirits that may be lodged in this area. Then command the loosing of these spirits and have them removed. You can do this by the power and authority that Jesus Christ has given you in His name.

Stroke

Physically:

Here is a little more information regarding how a stroke can affect the brain. When a stroke takes place, it arises from a restriction of blood flow to the brain where the blood cannot get to the region of the brain in charge of certain body functions. As a result, that part of the body will not work like it is supposed to.

If the stroke occurs toward the back of the brain, it's likely that some disability involving vision will occur. The different effects will be dependent on what kind of obstruction took place, what side it took place on, and to what extent of the brain tissue was affected.

If the incident happened on the right side you may come across problems such as paralysis of the left side of the body, vision problems, quick inquisitive behavioral style, and memory loss. On the left side of the brain you may see similar effects take place on the right side of your body such as the paralysis. You may also see memory loss. However if the left side is damaged, you could have speech and language problems as well as a slow, cautious behavior style.

The brain stem can affect a person on both sides of the body depending on the severity of the injury and may leave someone in a 'locked-in' state. When this happens a person is generally unable to speak or achieve any movement below the neck.

Spiritually:

So because there are different things that this can affect, please use this information to address different places in your body were spirits could be lodging. Realize that spirits can cause these issues as well to make it seem like you have had an actual stroke when you may not had one at all.

It is important to know your family history so that you can pray against any type of repeats in the family line, family curses, medical problems, generational trauma, etc. If you do not know these things, just ask the Holy Spirit and He will show you.

It would also be wise to pray health in these areas. Break any generational curses and cast out any generational spirits in this area if you have found this to run in your family. Break it off of your children and children's children. If you do not know about generational curses and spirits I would highly suggest to research it because a lot of health problems can come from these types of things. You can do this with any other disease or sickness that has repeated in your blood line.

On the spiritual side of things, think about how many times you have seen people stuck in a certain state due to traumatic events or accidents in their spiritual walks, especially those who have been extremely wounded by the Body of Christ. When this takes place, it would be ideal to pray and ask God if He can reveal if this person has suffered a spiritual stroke and how to handle it.

I would encourage anyone reading this book that experiences the symptoms of a stroke to first seek professional medical advice by a certified healthcare provider to prevent any further injury.

The enemy wants to paralyze you in any way he can to stop you from fulfilling your destiny in God. A spirit of sabotage and witchcraft may be lurking and have to be dealt with. Remember these spirits do not want you to know that they are there because they do not want you to abort their assignments over you. Rebuke the spirit of death and speak creation and life as God has written it in your book in heaven that He has written about you.

Hebrews 10:7 (NIV)
Then I said, 'Here I am—it is written about me in the scroll—I have come to do your will, my God.'"

Psalm 139:16 (NIV)
Your eyes saw my unformed body; all the days ordained for me were written in your book before one of them came to be.

If you have already suffered a stroke or know someone who has, pray and petition God in the Courts for the person's healing. Read healing Scriptures from the Word of God to them. Speak encouragement and life into them. Do not count them out, or put them to the side. When you do this, you are allowing the enemy to succeed in his attempt to take the person out or to stop you from learning something that has left that person in your life. Really seek God's face over it and be open to what He has to say.

But you are also going to have to be very open to receive the whole truth. God may tell you that there is nothing you can do and you will have to leave it at that. When you go pass the threshold of going past what God has said to do, you end up seeing more damage than good being done. You are also saying you know better than God. Obedience and openness is the key to hearing what to do in situations such as these.

However if God has given you the "go ahead" to help this person or to pray over yourself, put your belief in Him and allow your faith to grow and see the healing take place. Nothing is too far gone unless God says it is. He is the one who creates and gives life. Don't be afraid to do your homework in this area. Seek God's Word and use it in the deepest capacity that you can. His Word never comes back void.

Isaiah 55:11 (NIV)

so is my word that goes out from my mouth: It will not return to me empty, but will accomplish what I desire and achieve the purpose for which I sent it.

Stroke – Reflection and Application:

A stroke takes place when the blood flow is restricted in the brain and the body cannot function as it is supposed to. The side effects of restricted blood flow to different regions of the brain are as follows:

Back: Visual impairment

Right side: Partial or full paralysis on the left side of your body, visual problems, spontaneous behavior style and or memory loss.

Left side: Partial or full paralysis on the right side of the body, speech and language impairment, precautionary behavior impairment and or memory loss.

Brainstem: The person may experience being in a "locked-in" state. Conscious and aware, but unable to communicate.

o List the family medical history:

o List other things in the family line such as traumas, accidents, or even spiritual failure or sin that has been repeated:

o Break all family curses, generational spirits and agreements, generational wounds, generational involvement in witchcraft and demonic religion, and things like this off of you and your future generations.

o Break off all spirits of paralysis, spirits of death, the infirmity of strokes off of you. Break all assignments that would cause your destiny to become aborted or paralyzed in the spiritual realm.

Parietal Lobe

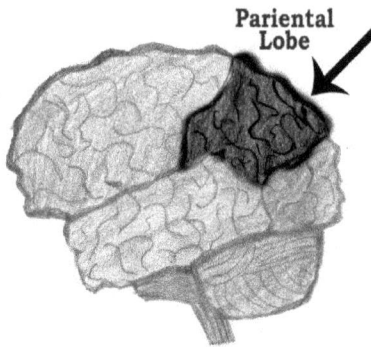

Pariental
Lobe

Physically:

Your parietal lobe function is to receive the sensations in skin, muscles, joints, and organs. Its function is also to receive information of body awareness, perception, attention and your language.

One of the main functions and responsibilities of the parietal lobe is the sense of touch. It has to be able to process sensory information within seconds. The parietal lobe is where information such as taste, temperature and touch are processed. If this area becomes damaged you would not be able to feel or taste.

Different areas of the parietal lobe are responsible for processing language without being verbal. This would be extremely important to someone who is physically blind and would need this lobe to help them communicate and understand in other areas. It would also make sense that this is also where physical pain is registered and being able to locate the point of pain by sense of touch. Also parietal lobe damage causes marked deficits in focus and perception.

Damage to the parietal lobe could show up in a person as having issues with difficulty reading, recognizing people and objects, and having a comprehensive awareness of his or her own body and limbs. You may find that the ability to do multiple things at the same time is reduced or eliminated.

Damage to the parietal lobe most often occurs as a result of vehicle crashes, falls, firearms, or other physical traumas. One of the possible effects of trauma is the inability to attend to more than one object at a time. In other words, you would not be able to multi-task. Other damages would include not being able to name an object, write words, or focus visual attention. This would also bring difficulties with drawing objects, distinguishing left from right, and not being fully aware of where certain body parts are in surrounding space, which makes it harder to being able to help take care of yourself in the normal activities of daily living.

With damages in the parietal lobe, you may also have difficulties in reading, math, and hand-eye coordination.

Spiritually:

There are times in ministry where we have come across those who have become numb in the spiritual and the physical realm. You become out of touch with things that should be felt, developing an inability to focus and comprehend what is going on. This may even come to the place where you feel completely unable to connect with reality.

In some cases we have seen people exposed to proper teaching and guidance, powerful moves of the Holy Spirit, and deep revelation poured into their spirit-man – yet the person cannot focus on the flow of the Spirit nor retain/operate in the revelation and anointing that is being poured into them.

There may come times where you feel that you have come out of touch with your feelings and sense of touch as if it was abruptly taken from you. The long term damage that can be done if not dealt with can become a way for the enemy to completely take you over with disillusion and cause you to suffer from not knowing what is real.

Using an example of how a person learns not to touch a hot stove, in a similar manner, the enemy could dull and numb your perception of pain and the automatic response to remove yourself from danger. The result would be a person actually being hurt and damaged but never perceiving the pain or danger of it; whereby destroying themselves spiritually – since they have no conviction or perception to flee or refrain from the act or environment.

Have there ever been times in the spirit where you have become numb and not able to feel things like you should? Have there been times that people have said they could feel the presence of God or sadness in the air but you could not?

This could possibly be a sign that in this area there can be walls and barriers built. There may be been some part of you that has been separated or damaged with your connection to the Spirit. You may very well feel cut off or empty when it comes to giving or receiving affection. Your compassion can be in captivity and be blocked and needs to be addressed in this area.

When spirits of infirmity produce any of these symptoms you are going to want to use the weapon of prayer to dislodge them and remove them. Then ask God to reverse the damage, restore, and make whole.

You are going to want to make sure you seek God's face, and ask Him if there are spirits that are hiding in there and where they are hiding that has caused the infirmity.

We have found with sickness and diseases, there are spirits of infirmity and other spirits that attach themselves to the person with the symptoms. These kinds of spirits will use these illnesses as a legal right to be there, shield themselves from being removed, or hide their presence. When praying for healing you will want to follow the "message of pain" to the source to get rid of the root. Remove all legal rights at the root and pull the roots up in the spirit realm to get rid of the spirits completely.

For example:

Tactile disorders, or sensory processing disorders, affect the sense of touch. It is rooted in the brain and central nervous system and may be the result of neural deregulation or from brain tumors, injury or surgery. Understanding the various tactile disorders sheds light on what is a very challenging issue to those who suffer from them and what area to target in the spirit realm.

There are links from this that are associated with people affected by autism. So this would be a good place to start praying health and wellness to this part of the brain and remove all demonic activity, so that you are only dealing with the actual illness and working with God for the physical healing.

There are too many times a person just thinks that they are not as intelligent as others. The truth is there very well could be more to it than that. It is time to examine all that is going on.

It is time to realize what weaknesses you have and seek God's face on how to get stronger in those areas even with your brain. Think about it with me for a second. If you are not good at math, but want to become better, you would practice and study and find out how you can learn it. It is no different than finding out your learning curve to defeat the enemy and have the spirits removed in your brain so that you can receive your complete healing and go forward in your walk with God whole.

Parietal Lobe – Reflection and Application:

The Parietal lobe is the receptor of the sensations felt in the skin, muscles, joints, organs, body awareness, perception, attention and your language. You receive the sense of touch, taste, and of temperature. This is where pain is registered. People who may have damage in this area may find they have difficulties in reading, math, and hand/eye coordination.

Take a look at your ministry of any kind. Do you notice if you have felt numb in the spiritual or physical sense, an inability to focus or comprehend what is going on, or unable to connect with reality? List the times that you have felt that and ask the Holy Spirit to reveal the root of it.

- o Removal of all disillusionment and false reality.

- o Unblock and break free all compassion that is in captivity.

- o Remove all spirits of infirmity.

Occipital Lobe

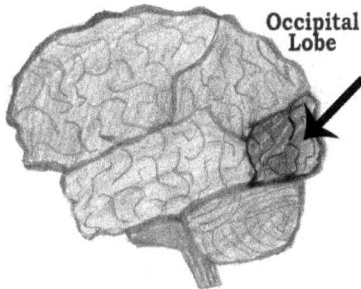

Occipital
Lobe

Physically:

The occipital lobe is located at the rear of your brain and behind the parietal and temporal lobes. The occipital lobe is responsible for your eyes to see and process information from the eyes. The occipital lobe is also responsible for recognition of shapes and color. This lobe is where the brain receives input from the retina in the eye. In other words, this lobe has to work swiftly so that it can process the continuous information quickly that comes in from our eyes. Think of it as the visual processor of the brain.

The occipital lobe is similar to the temporal lobe except for the eyes instead of the ears. It is where images are formed once the information has been analyzed. The occipital lobe is the art that receives the nerve impulses of the eye. If it was injured or damaged it would make it difficult to process the visual signals which would then cause visual confusion.

The occipital lobe has different areas connected to visual communication. One area is where visual images of language are received. This is known as the visual receiving area. Another area is where it is interpreted or comprehended. This is known as the visual association area.

It is extremely important for reading and reading comprehension. Being able to read with accuracy is important in conducting one's affairs of life and activities of daily living.

An example: If you could only read English and you saw something written in another language you would only see the words, not understand them. This is using the visual receiving area only and not the visual association area.

When you have damage to the occipital lobe, it will most likely to result in visual impairments and other vision-related problems. Believe it or not, even if both eyes are functioning normally, if both sides are damaged, people cannot see. This disorder is called cortical blindness. Some people with cortical blindness are unaware that they cannot see. Imagine what that must be like.

If the back part is damaged, people have difficulty recognizing familiar objects and faces and accurately interpreting what they see. They are usually unaware of their problem and often make up descriptions of what they see. Their false descriptions are their "reality". These are symptoms of Anton-Babinski syndrome.

Different symptoms you might see of having damage to your occipital lobe would be a difficulty with locating objects in the environment, difficulty with identifying colors, word blindness (inability to recognize words), difficulty in recognizing drawn objects, and difficulties with reading and writing.

You will also find that you can have damage to your vision such as defects in vision, production of hallucinations, visual illusions (inaccurately seeing objects, an example a mirage), and inability to recognize the movement of object. Keep these in mind as you approach the occipital lobe in the spirit realm.

Spiritually:

Spiritually this lobe can be a major area when it comes to your spiritual sight and comprehension of the Word of God and being a doer of the Word and not just a seer/reader. If you are having cloudiness of vision, fogginess of seeing in the spiritual realm it would be a good idea to really press in to have the spirits removed and all devices that could be blocking your occipital lobe.

2 Timothy 1:7 (KJV)
For God hath not given us the spirit of fear; but of power, and of love, and of a sound mind.

It could also be the place spirits are hiding when you are only seeing half of what you are shown and not understanding it. It would be an impairment. It could come in the forms of reading, visions, dreams, people, etc. This would be an important lobe to keep extremely clean if you are a seer which is one who "sees" spiritual pictures and carries the seer's anointing.

Praying to remove all spiritual blindness in the spiritual realm would also require this area to be cleansed so that there is nothing hindering and the area is completely clean from demonic activity. If you are walking in spiritual confusion, delusion, discouragement, doubt, or anything similar, this would be a good area to shine the Light of Jesus in. He will remove the darkness that is causing you to walk in the mindsets of these spirits.

John 8:12 (KJV)
Then spake Jesus again unto them, saying, I am the light of the world: he that followeth me shall not walk in darkness, but shall have the light of life.

When the Light of Jesus is shone into your visions it strengthens it and allows you to have clarity instead of confusion about what you are seeing. If you are looking through wounds of the soul then you are going to comprehend through those wounds. That is why it is so important to be healed of your soul wounds so that you interpret what you are seeing correctly.

Psalm 19:8 (KJV)
The statutes of the Lord are right, rejoicing the heart: the commandment of the Lord is pure, enlightening the eyes.

If this area is damaged, you may become blinded without knowing it. An example of spirits that would cause you damage and problems in this area are spirits of delusion and deception. It really puts a new perspective on people who really do not know what they are doing at times and think that you are the one who is crazy. It is better to pray healing to this gland in order to see the vision become clear whilst removing the spirits of delusion and deception.

You can also pray for healing in this area for yourself when it comes to having visual impairments and speak wholeness to your occipital lobe so that not only can you think better, but you can see well also. For example, if you happened to be color blind you could pray for the cones on the retina of your eyes as well as the communication and receivers to the occipital lobe.

Occipital Lobe – Reflection and Application:

The occipital lobe deals with the eyesight, recognizing shapes and colors and processing the continuous flow of information that is received from our eyes. Go through this list and see if you have suffered from any of these:

Physical checklist:

- o Cortical blindness (unaware that you cannot see)
- o Difficulty recognizing familiar objects and faces
- o Difficulty accurately interpreting what you see
- o Difficulty with locating objects in the environment
- o Difficulty with identifying colors
- o Word blindness
- o Inability to recognize words
- o Difficulty in recognizing drawn objects
- o Difficulty with reading and writing
- o Defects in vision
- o Production of hallucinations
- o Inaccurately seeing objects (like in a mirage)
- o Inability to recognize the movement of objects

Spiritual checklist:

- o Cloudiness of spiritual vision
- o Fogginess seeing in the spiritual realm
- o Only seeing half of the picture
- o Dreams, visions, prophetic words, etc. – not being able to understand them
- o Blockage in the seer's anointing or gift
- o Confusion, delusion, discouragement and doubt
- o Lack of dreams and visions

The Light of Jesus strengthens your vision. Spiritually you are going to want to pray the Light of Jesus into your vision and remove the spirits of blindness, confusion, delusion, deception, etc. in the name of Jesus.

Thalamus

Medulla

The Brain Stem

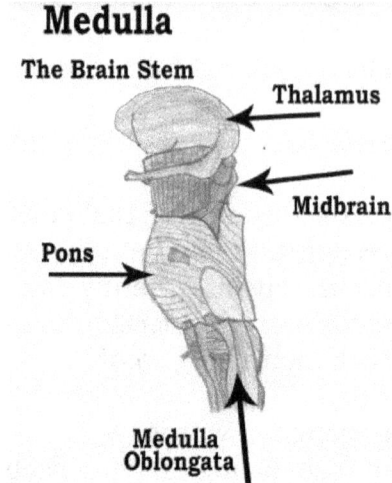

Thalamus

Midbrain

Pons

Medulla
Oblongata

Physically:

The thalamus is located within the brainstem. It is a part of the pathway of information into the cerebrum. This is the section of the brain that is responsible for thinking and movement. The thalamus is also responsible for detecting and relaying information from our senses, such as hearing and vision.

The thalamus is known as the center of your brain. It holds the sensory relay to the cortex and motor information. It is responsible for relaying those messages from the sensory receptors to the proper areas of the brain where it can be processed.

There are 12 pairs of Cranial Nerves that carry information from your senses to and from your brain and your body. It helps with the consciousness, sleep, and alertness. It also controls the motion, balance and ability to learn new things.

The thalamus is like the guide that distributes or identifies the different sensory information of four of the five senses that is being transmitted to the brain. The signals of the four senses include sight, touch, taste, and hearing. After it identifies it and diagnoses it, then it directs it to the correct location of parts and lobes of the cortex.

If something disruptive occurs in this part of the brain, sensory information would be damaged and sensory confusion would take place. It would be just like getting a wrong diagnosis from the doctor and failing to understand why things are not functioning correctly despite the treatment. You would be off-balance on your coordination and fine tuning.

There is an opinion among experts that the thalamus serves as a kind of gate, filtering which information from various channels is allowed to be relayed by it for processing. However, the thalamus is crucial for perception, with 98% of all sensory input being relayed by it. The only sensory information that is not relayed by the thalamus into the cerebral cortex is information related to smell.

So in summary, the thalamus analyzes different sensory information that is transmitted to the brain relating to hearing or sound, visual, relating to touch, and relating to taste signals. After this takes place, it redirects the information to different parts and lobes of the cortex. One symptom of damage to the thalamus is a persistent pain down one side of the body similar to a burning sensation after having a stroke.

Damage to the thalamus can be accompanied by a prickling sensation, or a sensation of tearing or of pressure. The pain ranges from mild to excruciating and can be changed or magnified by cold or by touch.

Another experience of a damaged thalamus is the loss of feeling and even paralysis down one side of the body after a stroke. The feeling and motor control can often be regained, unlike the paralysis and loss of feeling that result from damage to the spinal cord.

Damage to the thalamus can also be seen in some movement disorders. These can be involved in dystonia, or involuntary muscle contractions.

Thalamic damage can also cause insomnia and other sleep disorders. The thalamus is deeply involved in the wake-sleep-wake cycle. Damage to the thalamus can permanently damage the ability to sleep.

Spiritually:

The thalamus would be an area where the gate of misunderstanding and misinterpretation could take place. If a spirit of confusion lodged itself in this area, it would open a door to complete chaos. It could mess up all the signals to know what you feel, touch, smell, see, etc. It would change your perceptions and misread information that is being brought to you, even by others.

When a person is being manipulated or deceived it very well could be a spirit in there having a heyday with the nerve connections and sensory transmission. Healing would need to take place by shining in the light of truth and see the damage that is being done, and reversing it. The 'gate' or filter needs to be cleansed and ask God to bring healing to these areas and complete function how He intended to take place.

This would also be a perfect hiding place for the spirit of restlessness to hide and cause a person to lose sleep. Losing sleep causes you to be "off your game" so to speak. Your body would not be able to function correctly and you could even become weakened and susceptible to the enemy's attacks.

Much of what I have read and researched and also from my personal experiences have shown that your body does not heal as well if you are not sleeping. You are unable to function properly and it spiritually drains the life out of you to have to fight. The enemy knows this and will use this strategy against you any chance he can.

If you find yourself having these problems, or problems of just feeling lazy, not seeing the whole picture, not feeling like you should, or feeling too much emotion, etc. then cast out the spirits of manipulation, deception, control, lethargy, and confusion. Ask God to strengthen you in this area and to shower rest upon you and endurance.

You are also going to want to attack every spirit of disunity and disorganization, strife and discord and dislodge them. Then ask God to reverse all damage as complete healing takes place. It would also be a wise thing to ask God that any damage you have caused upon others around you might be healed and that unity takes place.

You can also speak peace and clarity to the thalamus. You are also going to want to ask that each nerve connected is cleansed by the Blood of Jesus. Command each nerve connection to return to perfect working order. Command that the nerve connections become a shield of protection against anything the enemy would try to do to set up shop in this area to control your brain and anything attached to the brain.

Sometimes you may find yourself where you are off in the senses in the spirit realm. Just as your sense of smell would throw you off in the natural, it can do so in the spirit realm. Interlock what is going on in the natural realm with what is going on in the spirit realm and you will see that there is a much bigger picture going on. You will be able to see the connections and work on fixing them.

If you are experiencing these spiritual issues I can tell you that your best course of action would be to get someone else to pray over you and do deliverance on you. I say this because when you are walking in this deception and confusion, it is completely unclear to you that you are going through it and how severe it really is. If you live with someone, pay attention to what they say about you. Nine times out of ten they are hinting on a problem that they see exists and if you bring it to the Father in Heaven He will be able to help you change it.

Thalamus – Reflection and Application:

The thalamus is what is known as the center of the brain. It helps with the consciousness, sleep and alertness. It also controls the motion, balance and ability to learn new things. After the sense is assessed and identified, then it is directed to the correct location of the parts and lobes of the cortex. The thalamus acts as a gate, filtering which information from different places is allowed to be relayed for processing. It is very crucial for perception.

If damage occurred in this area you would experience being 'off your rocker' so to speak. Symptoms of damage could include but are not limited to:

- o Constant pain down one side of body, like a burning sensation or loss of feeling/paralyzed on one side of body – both can show up for several weeks after suffering a stroke
- o Prickling sensation
- o Sensation of tearing or pressure
- o Pain can be magnified or changed by cold or touch
- o Some muscle disorders – dystonia, involuntary muscle contractions
- o Insomnia and other sleeping disorders – can even become a permanent problem of not being able to sleep

Are you easy to be manipulated or deceived and your signals are all messed up?

Do you find yourself having problems with misunderstandings and misinterpretations?

Have you found yourself lazy and your sleep is all messed up or unable to sleep at all?

Have you been feeling like you are not seeing the whole picture; that information seems to not be going in the right direction to give you what you need to see the picture?

Have you been feeling not quite yourself or have you been feeling like you are feeling too much emotion?

If you have answered yes, then you are going to want to remove from the gates of the thalamus: misunderstanding and misinterpretation, and cast out the following spirits by the leading of the Holy Spirit and by the name of Jesus Christ:

Spirits of confusion	Manipulation	Deception
Control	Lethargy	Restlessness
Disunity	Disorganization	Strife
Discord	Misunderstanding	
Misinterpretation	Insomnia	

Reverse the damage and shine the Light of Jesus and speak healing into these areas and cleanse the gates. Speak peace and clarity into your thalamus and that each connection is cleansed and working in proper order to receive and transmit the proper information for normal functioning both physically and spiritually.

Cerebellum

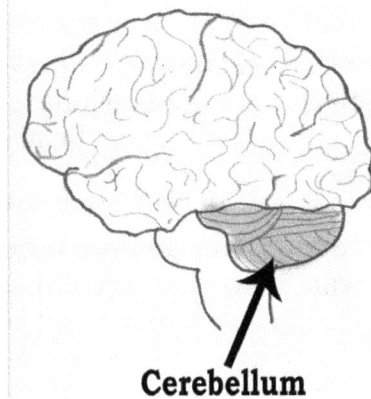

Cerebellum

Physically:

The cerebellum is also known as the little brain. Its key role is motor control, coordination, and special navigation, which is how to tell the distance of an object. The cerebellum is the area found at the back and bottom of the brain and behind the brainstem. The cerebellum is responsible for balance and coordination of your muscles and the body. It does several things which include: coordinating movement, vision, motor learning, and other functions such as thinking including thoughts related to language and mood.

The cerebellum is also responsible for accurate timing and precision. It receives input from the sensory system of the spinal cord and other parts of the brain and integrates this information to fine-tune motor activity.

This part of the cerebellum is what helps you do everyday tasks such as walking and writing. It is also what helps you be able to stay balanced and upright. When the cerebellum is not functioning correctly people can have disorders in fine movement, posture, and even motor learning. The symptoms of the cerebellum not working properly can show up as lack of muscle control and coordination, difficulty walking, slurred speech, difficulty speaking, abnormal eye movements and headaches.

You will see that these signs and symptoms are seen because they involve a disturbance in muscle control. Some of the disorders of the cerebellum would include but are not limited to strokes, brain bleeding, toxins, genetic malformations, infection, and cancer.

To keep it from becoming damaged you need to keep your brain healthy. You can reduce the risk of these disorders by quitting smoking, limiting alcohol use and keeping yourself involved in physical activities such as exercising. It is good to exercise at least 2.5 hours a week.

You can also reduce the risk of the disorders by protecting the head and following multiple safety guidelines that you are taught throughout your life such as wearing a seat belt or bike helmet. Preventing falls is very important, no matter the age. Children must be properly supervised to prevent falls from heights caused by their natural curiosity and lack of fear. Another preventive measure would be to avoid handling lead. Lead is no longer used in new construction, but older homes may have lead pipes and paint (lead paint was banned by Congress in 1971 but wasn't fully enforced until 1978 by the Consumer Product Safety Commission). This is one of the reasons why it is important to have your baby tested for lead between the ages of 1 and 2 years old. I know for me personally I did not understand why my pediatrician wanted this test. I can say that by coming across this information and learning about the brain, it is a very important test that they are asking for and for very good reasoning.

Spiritually:

So what could this mean spiritually? You may find when you have spiritual issues in the area of the cerebellum that you can have the inability to see clearly and possibly have pressure in your head or headaches from when you study the Word of God, or are doing things for God's kingdom in ministry.

With the spiritual cerebellum you would also want to be lined up with the will of God. You would want your spiritual cerebellum to be coordinated with Him so that the functioning of your spiritual muscles is working properly. You are also going to want to make sure that you ask God to remove all blockages that could be there to stop your spiritual brain from receiving the proper information from other areas of your body and brain.

The spiritual cerebellum is important to keep in balance because you could be thrown off balance and have the inability to walk the correct path with God without stumbling and falling. There may be times when you start "tripping" over your words or start having a hard time being able to speak or express what you are trying to say.

When you find yourself in these situations you can ask Him to help you convey what you are speaking of and then leave the rest in God's hands. Ask God to clean any miscommunication in the line and clear up your voice that He has given you. And ask God to heal anything that may be going on in the cerebellum whether it be physical or spiritual that is causing you to have these speaking problems. If you have or are praying for someone who had physical or spiritual cancer, strokes, or anything effecting the speech, pray against all spirits of cancer and of strokes and any damage that has happened from having one. There is hope of restoration of these areas in Jesus Christ.

When dealing with spiritual cancer and spiritual strokes you are going to want to stay in tune to the Holy Spirit and ask Him how the spirits have affected this area. Each individual can be different.

You are also going to want to pray and remove the following out of your spiritual cerebellum:
   a. Remove all toxins
   b. Stop any and all brain bleeding, physical and spiritual
   c. Remove all genetic malformations and all generational curses and illness to go with it
   d. Treat ALL infections

When you pray these things away, it would be very wise to ask God to install some gear to keep you safe in case you fall. And when you fall you are able to recover quickly, realizing everyone has stumbled and fell at some time.

Romans 3:22-24 (NIV)
22 This righteousness is given through faith in Jesus Christ to all who believe. There is no difference between Jew and Gentile,
23 for all have sinned and fall short of the glory of God,
24 and all are justified freely by his grace through the redemption that came by Christ Jesus.

One other thing you are going to want to pray is to remove all spiritual toxic lead. Remove all old doctrines that would cause one to have a mindset of religion and not about the kingdom of God.

Colossians 2:8 (NIV)
See to it that no one takes you captive through hollow and deceptive philosophy, which depends on human tradition and the elemental spiritual forces of this world rather than on Christ.

Remove all things from the old house that is toxic and worldly things that could contaminate and weigh you down.

Ask God to tear down and destroy anything that you have built upon that was not on Jesus Christ and repair your foundation. If you do not do this it will become just like the man who built upon the sand, and it will fall.

You will see that as you press in further you will understand why we are to pay attention to our balance, our ability to move correctly, and to work with a clear mind. It is important to be able to have a mind that is not held down in bondage.

When you are not functioning correctly it leaves the door open to discouragement, frustration and an inability to do daily tasks. It brings in mindsets of failure and begins to damage your spiritual muscles and ability to strive moving forward.

You are going to want to pray against this so that you can have a clear and open channel to the Heavenly Father. Speak life and restoration into your spiritual cerebellum. Command them to come into balance and line up to the Word of God.

Exercise your spiritual cerebellum as you are communicating with God and to others about God. Allow God to heal all areas that have become infected. When balance comes into play you will be able to walk with more confidence and assurance that everything is working correctly.

Cerebellum – Reflection and Application:

The cerebellum is known as the little brain. Its key role is motor control, coordination, special navigation (telling the distance of an object), responsible for balance and coordination in the muscles and body, accurate timing and precision, and helps you do everyday activities such as walking and writing, and helps you stay balanced and upright.

When it is damaged you could have disorders in fine movement, posture, and motor learning. Symptoms can be things like lack of control of muscles and coordination, difficulty walking, slurred speech, difficulty speaking, abnormal eye movements and headaches. Disorders can include but are not limited to: strokes, brain bleeding, toxins, genetic malformations, infections and cancer.

Spiritual Checklist:

- o Inability to see clearly
- o Headache when studying the Word
- o Headache when doing things for God
- o Thrown off balance in spiritual walk
- o Inability to walk the correct path
- o Miscommunication when speaking
- o Inability to speak
- o Spiritual cancer
- o Spiritual stroke

Spiritual Treatment:

1. Remove all toxins
2. Stop any brain bleeds (physical and spiritual)
3. Remove all genetic malformations
4. Remove all generational curses
5. Remove all generational illnesses
6. Removal of old doctrines (mindsets of religion)
7. Spiritual toxic lead
8. Removal of contamination
9. Removal of worldly things and weights
10. Removal of anything built that is not on Jesus
11. Removal of mindsets of failure
12. Removal of spirits of leviathan
13. Removal of mute spirit
14. Removal of the spirits of the wanderer, wayward and prodigal

And any other spirit that the Holy Spirit reveals to remove it in the name of Jesus.

To exercise your spiritual cerebellum is to communicate with God and to others about God.

Medulla (Brain Stem)

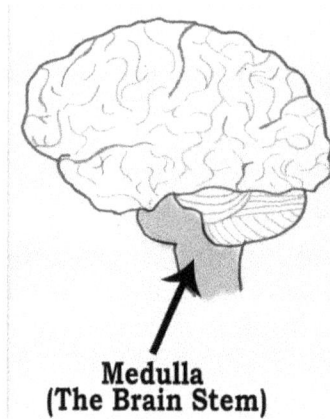

**Medulla
(The Brain Stem)**

Physically:

The brain stem is one of the most vital regions for the body's survival. It is the connection between the brain and the spinal cord. It is the nerve pathway that runs all the way down your back sending and receiving communication and information from the senses.

The brainstem also maintains vital control of the heart and lungs. It is a major lifeline in your body and the need to understand its role is very important. The brainstem also coordinates many important reflexes. Some of these reflexes are involuntary. It manages vital functions such as breathing, circulation, sleeping, digestion, and swallowing. The vital survival reflexes include vomiting, sneezing, and coughing.

There are three major regions that make up the brain stem: medulla oblongata, pons, and the midbrain.

The medulla oblongata which is located at lowest part of the brainstem contains control centers for the heart and lungs. It is what regulates the involuntary actions such as your heart beat and digestion. It also contains the cardiovascular center that controls the heart rate and blood pressure, and the medullary rhythmicity area. The rhythmicity is what controls the breathing rate.

The pons contains all the neurons that connect the higher regions of the brain to the medulla and spinal cord. It plays a vital role in communication. The pons acts as a bridge in these crucial ways. It connects the left and right hemispheres of the cerebellum to one another, and it connects the cerebellum to the other regions of the brain.

The midbrain is in the center part of the brainstem. It also plays important roles in communication and in the control of the motor system, vision and hearing, and the reflexes related to visual and auditory stimuli. The brainstem also encases the nerve system that regulates the respiration, blood pressure, bladder control, and it is extremely important in maintaining consciousness and regulating the sleep cycle. It also regulates the central nervous system.

Spiritually:

The brain stem is one area the enemy will target to coil and entangle spirits, devices, control and infirmities so that it can have access to multiple areas in the body. It is like an entry way in both directions.

Personally I have witnessed and experienced multiple times where spirits have been lodged in this area. When these are cast out and things are removed there has been immediate results of relief and change takes place both physically and spiritually.

This is where there has been built up stress, spiritual snakes coiled, bodies paralyzed in areas trying to shut the body down, and even having a hard time holding your head up correctly. We have cast out numerous spirits from this area and removed many devices in the spirit realm from this area.

There has been multiple times where the nerves have been addressed in this area and the person was set free of the pain and was able to breathe easier.

If you are having problems with your nerves, you can address this area in the spirit realm and send the healing power of God down each and every nerve path and go to the place of pain and have it targeted and addressed. This includes the pain in the back. If your senses are not responding as they should, you can pray and ask that the brain stem is corrected and lined up with the way God has created it to be made and to function properly.

The brain stem is connected to both the lung and heart functions. So when your heart and lungs are not working properly, you can pray over this area. For your lungs you can command your body to breathe correctly as your body has been created to breathe. Command the area of rhythmicity to have your breathing rate to be correct for the body to receive the correct oxygen level that your body needs to be healthy.

For your heart, you can command your circulation to be regulated. You can command your heart beat to be tuned to the blueprints that God created it to beat. Each person has a unique rhythm that God has placed inside of us known as God's heart song. Line up your heart beat with God's personal song for you for the function of your body.

You can also command your blood pressure to normalize and to stay that way. Command every spirit of anxiety, fear, discouragement, disappointment, frustration, anger and anything else the Holy Spirit brings to your attention to leave in the name of Jesus. You can command every sickness, disease, infection, toxin, and anything else the enemy may have placed there to destroy your heart to go the pit in Jesus' name.

If you are having problems sleeping and getting the proper sleep that is not due to life's circumstances, you can address your brainstem to be relieved of all tensions and to relax and receive peace. You can command your body to maintain the correct sleeping cycle and the correct conscious cycle and bring balance so that you are able to contain the peace that you are to walk in.

The brainstem is also the area you can pray for if your body is not functioning correctly when it comes to sneezing, swallowing, coughing, vomiting, bladder control, digestions, and to regulate your central nervous system.

As you can see your brainstem is a place where many things can be addressed and most of them are due to fear, stress, depression, anger, etc. The neck is where the head and body are connected and without it neither the body nor the head can function nor live. If you suffer from fear, stress, anger, etc. pay attention to your neck and the tension in your neck. As you pray for your neck you will feel that God will go in and relieve the stress tension and you will feel much better. But don't stop at the neck. Be sure to include your brain stem so that every area is addressed.

Ask the Holy Spirit to go down each nerve path and sensor and ask to reveal the root of the problem and the location of the problem. Ask the Holy Spirit to go down and remove and reveal anything that is not correct and is causing problems. When you go to do this it would be advised to have something to write down the things you hear.

When you ask the Holy Spirit to do this, do so with openness and a mindset ready to receive what is being said. God will show you and sometimes it will not make sense. God is the Creator and knows all things and you are going to have to take Him for His Word as it is being spoken. After you have collected what God has said, you can look up what you heard and you will find that it will make sense. If you are still not at peace with it, then go to a person you trust to hear God and get confirmation. There is nothing wrong with doing that.

Think about it this way, if you were to go to the doctor, the doctor is going to give you terms that you may not understand and you have to look more into it. God is the Great Physician and it is the same way. Ask the Holy Spirit to help you in the researching also. Get into the Word and find what Scriptures you can use to bring forth healing into those areas that have been revealed.

Even though your brainstem seems small and a lot of time people do not think about it, but it is very important. Just like in the physical realm it has many important jobs that keep things running. Really seek God in this area and you may be surprised in what He shows you.

Medulla (The Brain Stem) – Reflection and Application:

The brain stem is a vital region for the body's survival.

Functions of the Brain Stem:
The brain stem is a vital control center of the heart and lungs; it coordinates many important reflexes, manages vital functions such as breathing, circulation, sleeping, digestion and swallowing. It also manages vital survival reflexes including vomiting, sneezing and coughing. Three major regions of the brain stem include: the medulla oblongata, pons and midbrain.

Medulla Oblongata:
The control center for the heart and lungs; regulates heart beat and digestion, controls the heart rate and blood pressure, and the medullary rhythmicity area (breathing rate).

Pons:
Connects the higher regions of the brain to the medulla and spinal cord; vital role in communication, connects the left and right hemispheres of the cerebellum, connects the cerebellum to the other regions of the brain.

Midbrain:
Has important roles in communication; control of the motor system, vision and hearing and the reflexes related to visual and auditory stimuli.

The brainstem also encases the nerve system that regulates the respiration, blood pressure, bladder control and it is extremely important in maintaining consciousness and regulating the sleep cycle. It also regulates the central nervous system.

This may be a source of investigation if you have noticed that you have had issues with your brain stem, back problems, neck problems, heart and lung problems, nerve problems and the like. Here are things to remember and a check list that you can go through as you pray for healing and deliverance.

Remember:
The enemy will target to coil and entangle spirits, devices, control, and infirmities at the brain stem as an entry way to get to other areas of your body. It is like a channel of a river to streams. It is important to keep your brain stem clear and clean and the gate guarded.

In the brainstem you can find built up stress, spiritual snakes coiled, bodies paralyzed, shutting the body down, and having a hard time holding your head up.

Check List:

- Holy Spirit to go down every nerve path and go to the place of pain and address the pain. Command your body to breathe correctly and your breathing rate to be correct
- Command circulation to be regulated
- Command heart beat to line up with God's personal song for you
- Command your blood pressure to normalize
- Command every spirit of anxiety, fear, discouragement, disappointment, frustration, anger, stress and depression to be removed and cast out to the pit
- Command every sickness, disease, infection, toxin, and anything else the enemy may destroy the heart with to go the pit
- Command that the brainstem is relieved of all tensions and the neck relieved of the stress tension
- Command the brainstem to relax and receive peace
- Command the body to maintain the correct sleeping cycle
- Command the correct conscious cycle to be active when it is designed to and bring balance so peace is contained

God is the Great Physician. Use the Word of God by looking up the Scriptures and using them to bring alignment and balance to your body and seeing your body, soul and spirit become whole as you cleanse the brainstem spiritually.

The Limbic System

Physically:

The limbic system is a set of structures in the brain. These structures deal with emotions (such as anger, happiness and fear) as well as memories. It plays an important part in regulating emotions. It is what processes our emotions and drive. The limbic system also deals with the functions of memories and arousal (or stimulation).

The limbic system contains a reward circuit that releases a chemical called dopamine. It motivates you to repeat important body behaviors such as eating, having fun with friends, and falling in love.

When the limbic system experiences an artificial reward it can encourage risky behaviors that have brought these artificial rewards, such as taking drugs. This is because drugs cause a release of a higher level of dopamine (a high). When this takes place to get that "high" or pleasure from the dopamine release, it makes it harder to enjoy normal and simple pleasures, and continues to influence you to desire the artificial stimulation and release. It repeats the activation of the reward pathway that leads to the addiction.

Just as this happens with someone who is on drugs, it also happens with those who are involved with pornography, over eating, or anything that brings a gratification that is desired to be repeated.

When these things are distorted due to things such as sin and bad behavior, an imbalance takes place. A craving for the artificial imbalanced behavior increases. This is how additions are formed.

You can relate the limbic system to the same as you can with neural pathways.

Neural pathways in the brain also help form "grooves" or "ruts" in the areas of our brain that affect memory, recollection, and habits. This is what our brain is programmed to do and it is the first place it seeks when evoking a response or reaction.

Grooves and ruts in the wiring of our brain become deeper and more solid the longer the habit is repeated and such a thing becomes second-nature to a person. This applies to habits, routines, and initial responses.

Think of this like digging a trench that winds through your backyard. If you pour water out over the ground, chances are the water is going to primarily fill up the trench and follow it wherever it leads. It is difficult for the water to flow elsewhere besides the trench and equally as difficult to jump out of it.

So it is with a habit in the mind. New ruts have to be formed to slowly channel water in a new direction over a period of time. In the mind, it takes on average of two weeks to break a bad habit and form a new one. Neural pathways must be deconstructed while creating and practicing new habits.

Try this for yourself: Move your kitchen trash can to a different location for two weeks. Note how many times you keep going instinctively to the old location – and how long it takes you before that instinct is preprogrammed.

You have to do the same thing. A constant repeated pattern needs to take place in order to change the bad habits and stimulations and transform your mind. You are reprogramming your mind and bringing it back to balance.

The limbic system is made up of the hypothalamus, amygdala, thalamus, hippocampus, and it sits above the brain stem.

Spiritually:

The limbic system is a target area where the enemy brings havoc and causes chaos in a person. Not only are you dealing with the emotions of anger, happiness, fear, etc. and the memories along with it but this would be a place where great pain would be stored and spirits would be hidden and lodged in.

It is the place where imbalance can throw off the entire person's beliefs and actions. The limbic system is one of the major places that are affected by sin and needs to be transformed by the habits and behaviors to stop so the sin ceases.

The limbic system is one of the biggest playgrounds for the enemy. The kind of spirits that you may find hidden in there is lust, idolatry, adultery, fantasy, perversion, gluttony, fornication, jezebel, mammon, and other controlling spirits. It is where you will find spirits with addictive behaviors such as alcoholism and drug and tobacco addictions along with spirits of thievery and criminal behaviors. These are just the beginning of what hides itself in there.

If you have come across a person who suppresses their feeling this would be a place where it is collected and causes a blockage in their ability to process them. It is also where you want to break all the connections of feelings/emotions on the memories and remove the triggers.

Have you ever known someone who has been into perversion and wonder why just seeing the tops of a woman's breasts in a shirt would cause the man to react in a lustful manner when it doesn't seem like it would? This is because the man has associated that visual with a certain feeling. When they see that visual it triggers the feeling and causes a repeated behavior.

This is also where nail biting and different bad habits would be associated to different types of emotions. Bad habits turn into addictions. If you have ever known someone who bites their nails and asked them why they do it, most of the time they are not even aware they are doing it. It is usually also associated when the person is really concentrating on something or has anxiety of some sort. So what happens is your limbic system makes a memory with that emotion and brings forward the behavior.

Let us look at it in another way: a person who feels condemnation when being corrected could cause a trigger to be activated and react out of offense and shut down emotionally. Then whatever they do to relieve themselves from the condemnation is what they will resort to. Examples may be the nail biting previously mentioned, or food, addictions, and fantasy realms, etc. A good way to find out what are your triggers and associations with emotions is what do you do or where do you turn if you are feeling one way or another.

If a person's limbic system associates anger and rage into abuse and hitting, then it will be one of the first responses that will come to that person. This is why steps of reprogramming the bad habit into healthy habits is one of the biggest suggestions of self-help programs. The only issue with those is that they leave out the Great Physician, Jesus. Only Jesus can get to the very nitty gritty and make it a permanent change that is complete.

As dopamine was mentioned in the physical, in the limbic system, the dopamine itself is a chemical that is released for the brain to associate with pleasure or a high. When you are working with a person or praying for yourself you are going to want to ask God to regulate your dopamine levels and cleanse your mind from all memories that were made due to artificially stimulated release of the dopamine. When you do this you will find that any addiction is much easier to overcome.

You can also address the addictions at this part of your brain and remove all spirits attached to them. It is also a good idea to ask God to remove the effects of the reward system of the addiction and sin. When you are no longer feeling the rewards of these things it is much easier to let go. But if the reward system is not addressed then relapse and cravings are most likely recur.

We are going to break it down a little bit and shine some light of truth upon the areas in the limbic system and what the spirits have been up to and how to get it restored, leveled, and cleaned.

The Limbic System – Reflection and Application:

The limbic system is made up of the hypothalamus, amygdala, thalamus, hippocampus and sits above the brain stem. The limbic system is a set structure that deals with regulating and processing emotions, such as anger, happiness, fear, and the functions of memories and arousal drive or stimulations.

Dopamine is found in the limbic system. Dopamine is what motivates you to repeat body behaviors such as eating, having fun with friends and falling in love.

When the limbic system experiences artificial reward it encourages the pattern to repeat due to activating the reward pathway. This leads to addictions such as pornography, over eating or anything that brings a gratification.

The limbic system can be distorted due to sin and bad behavior. Artificial imbalances of behavior increases and addictions are formed.

Reward pathways form grooves and ruts in the brain that affect memory, recollection, habits, routines and responses that are formed.

It takes about 2 weeks to break a bad habit and form a new one. You can do that by deconstructing bad habits in the neural pathways while creating and practicing new, healthier habits.

Imbalance can throw off the entire person's beliefs and actions. The limbic system is one of the major places that are affected by sin and needs to be transformed by the habits and behaviors to stop so the sin ceases. A constant repeated pattern needs to take place in order to change the bad habits and stimulations so that your mind can be transformed.

When you do this you are reprogramming your mind to do what is correct and bringing it back to balance. But you must include Jesus with this process to get to the nitty gritty for the change to be permanent and complete.

Bad habits turn into addictions. Most of the time, people are not even aware they are doing it.

Prayer Check List:

Rebuke and cast out these spirits:
- Lust
- Idolatry
- Adultery
- Fantasy
- Perversion
- Gluttony
- Fornication
- Jezebel
- Mammon
- Controlling spirits
- Spirits with addictive behaviors (alcoholism and drug and tobacco addictions, nail biting etc.)
- Spirits of thievery
- Spirits of criminal behaviors
- Break all the connections of feelings/emotions on the memories that causes the addictions and bad behaviors
- Remove the triggers.
- Ask God to regulate your dopamine levels.
- Cleanse your mind from all memories that were made due to artificial stimulated release of the dopamine.
- Address the addictions at the limbic system.
- Remove the effects of the reward system of the addiction and sin.

List anything else that God reveals to you to include in your prayers and seeking deliverance for these things.

Hippocampus

Physically:

The hippocampus is another part of the limbic system and is also part of the temporal lobe. The hippocampus helps with the role of merging information from short-term memory to long-term memory.

The hippocampus helps in the role in forming new memories and in the detection of new surroundings, occurrences and being stimulated. The hippocampus does not necessarily help with the memories involved in learning a procedure, which are done by other areas in the brain.

The hippocampus also helps with the role in spatial memory that enables navigation. Spatial memory is memorizing landmarks and things in your environment. The spatial memory helps to be able to take you where you need to go. It also aids in figuring out how to get there with making the correct decisions based upon what you have already known or have found out or by memorizing.

The spatial memory of the hippocampus also helps you remember the positioning of items. For example you would be using this memory in the hippocampus when you would be recalling how to put things in a certain order when setting the table.

Someone with a strong spatial memory in the hippocampus may prefer to learn through visual and pictures. This would help them to be able to remember and relate it to memory for future experience if needed to repeat easier then audibly.

The hippocampus is involved in the storage of long-term memory. This includes all past knowledge and experiences.

Damage to the hippocampus can also result from oxygen starvation, and extensive hippocampal damage may be experienced by the inability to form and retain new memories.

Damage to the hippocampus can lead to loss of memory and difficulty in establishing new memories. The hippocampus is one of the first areas of the brain to be affected with Alzheimer's disease. When it is affected it leads to the confusion and loss of memory so commonly seen in the beginning stages of the disease.

Damage to the hippocampus can also show effects such as the ability to respond correctly and with the direction that has previously been learned. Many people with Alzheimer's or those who had issues with lack of oxygen to the brain will begin to lose their memory of where they live or even what they are doing. They may even have a hard time with remembering the past and this can bring much confusion on who they are and what they know. It can make them feel very frustrated and agitated because they cannot recollect what they know they knew before. All of this is directly affected by the hippocampus.

Spiritually:

Spiritually, if the hippocampus is blocked or hindered, you may find people being locked in their memories of the past and unable to escape from them. It may seem like they have a hard time making new memories. Walls of the past will have to be addressed and torn down. Prison cells of the mind will have to be destroyed and lined up with new ones that work properly.

This would be where you would have to seek God's face and ask Him if there is any blocking spirits, searing spirits of the mind, spirits of torture and spirits of pain, and other spirits that have made their "homes" in there. He will show you what would be blocking the person being prayed for that is stuck in the memories of the past and unable to make new ones.

Once He shows you and confirms that they are there, then you will have to listen intently to what the strategy is to tearing down the wall removing the strongholds, the strongman spirits, closing open doors, removing the gate keeper, and getting the root of why the walls were built in the first place.

Being stuck in your past memories is a horrible place to be because you are not able to move forward into the present or future. You are in a prison cell of what has been done that cannot be changed or controlled. The only way to get out of this cycle is to find out what has brought on the prison and have it destroyed.

Another spiritual issue you may find with a spiritually damaged hippocampus is the inability to familiarize yourself with what you are trying to learn that is a repeated or a necessary thing. You will find you are unable to put into your long term memory what you are learning and unable to pull it up when you need it. It makes it very difficult to make decisions that are necessary to go forward into the assignment or task that is at hand both physically and spiritually.

This would make any part of your walk with God hard as well as your walk in life and could bring on frustration and the sense of defeat. When you find that this is going on, you are going to need to rely on the Holy Spirit to do His part to draw it up from your spirit-man and to grow it in your heart, soul, and mind. In the Word, Jesus promised that He asked God the Father to send the Holy Spirit to do just that.

Do not stop reading the Word and attempting to learn. Continue to press through and pour in what you can and with God's help it will stick. Speak healing and pray protection over the seeds that are planted inside of you. Continue to water it with the presence of God and God's Word.

Persistence is needed to fill in the holes that the enemy may be draining out the information, wisdom and knowledge out of you. Also be seeking God's face and make sure you are not guilty of not fearing God (having a reverential respect for Him), not listening to God, not trusting God, not having a discerning heart but a foolish one, not walking in the Spirit of God and that is why you are losing out on the wisdom and knowledge that God has for you. All of this you can find in the Word of God:

Proverbs 1:7 (NIV)
The fear of the Lord is the beginning of knowledge, but fools despise wisdom and instruction.

Proverbs 1:29 (NIV)
since they hated knowledge and did not choose to fear the Lord.

Proverbs 2:6 (NIV)
For the Lord gives wisdom; from his mouth come knowledge and understanding.

Psalm 119:66 (NIV)
Teach me knowledge and good judgment, for I trust your commands.

Proverbs 18:5 (NIV)
It is not good to be partial to the wicked and so deprive the innocent of justice.

Proverbs 15:14 (NIV)
The discerning heart seeks knowledge, but the mouth of a fool feeds on folly.

Isaiah 11:2 (NIV)
The Spirit of the Lord will rest on him— the Spirit of wisdom and of understanding, the Spirit of counsel and of might, the Spirit of the knowledge and fear of the Lord—

When your spiritual hippocampus is damaged you will also find that it is hard to do things line upon line and precept upon precept. It will be hard to do things in order and correctly. Rebuke all spirits that are causing disorganization, and ask God to give you new and orderly mindsets that will get you on track and lined up according to His Will.

An important thing to know both spiritually and physically and that would be vital to your life is knowing how you learn and how you remember things. For some people it may be visual and with others it may be audible. If you find a hindrance in the way you learn that is a flag that needs to be prayed for. It can be addressed when praying for your hippocampus.

Another thing you can address for both your physical and spiritual hippocampus is your "core" long term memory. Ask God to remove all things of darkness and pain that have collected in your hippocampus. Ask God to remove all that has lodged itself in there that is not of Him.

Ask God to heal all broken memories that needs repairing. Request protection and speak life over your core memories. In others words, the core long term memory that God says needs to be there and are necessary for you to do and accomplish the calling you have on your life. Ask God that as you are guarding your heart, that your mind is also guarded and the connection between your mind and your heart.

More on Alzheimer's:

When praying for someone who has the infirmity of Alzheimer's or the symptoms of it, address the hippocampus.

Do this for both the physical and spiritual aspects of it. Address and rebuke the spirits of infirmity in the name of Jesus. Then address all the effects it has had on the hippocampus.

Rebuke the spirits of confusion, frustration, and agitation. Speak healing into the areas of memory loss and ask God to restore all the vital and necessary memory back. Speak life back into the areas to retain and gain the ability of keeping memory.

Ask God to bring strength into your sense of direction and that your purpose is restored into your life. Speak order and a sense of belonging. Speak organization back into your life and that it will come into fruition.

Ask God to amplify the Holy Spirit in all the areas that you are addressing. Pray that the ability of remembrance is restored. Also rebuke the spirits of insecurity, forgetfulness, and spirit of wanderer. Seek God's face and be sure to address anything that could be hereditary and generational for the infirmity to be there.

Hippocampus – Reflection and Application:

The hippocampus helps with the role of merging information from short-term memory to long-term memory and storing information in the long term memory. It is responsible for forming new memories, detection of new surroundings, occurrences and being stimulated, helps memorizing landmarks, things in your environment and remembers the positioning of items.

When there is damage to the hippocampus you may find the following symptoms and problems:

Oxygen deficiency, inability to form, retain, and establish new memories; loss of memory. Alzheimer's disease can be found in this region due to a lack of oxygen to the brain, and could possibly cause the person to begin to lose their memory of where they live or even what they are doing. Confusion takes place because they have a hard time remembering the past and this makes it difficult to know who they are and what they know and this brings on much frustration and agitation.

Others who have damage to their hippocampus can find themselves in mental prison cells, locked in their memories of the past, and unable to get out of them. They are walls of the past in the mind that brings destruction.

Application Check List:

Spirits to address, rebuke and cast out:

- o Blocking spirits
- o Searing spirits of the mind
- o Spirits of torture
- o Spirits of pain
- o Strongman spirits
- o Spirits of frustration
- o Spirits of discouragement and defeat
- o Tearing down the wall
- o Removing the strongholds
- o Closing open doors
- o Removing the gate keeper
- o The root of the walls
- o Pray for the ability to make decisions and focus to go forward into the assignment or task both physically and spiritually.
- o Pray for organization and new, orderly mindsets
- o Ask God to heal all broken memories
- o Request protection
- o Ask God that as you are guarding your heart that He also guards your mind and the connection between your mind and your heart.

Persistence is needed to fill in the holes that the enemy may be draining out the information, wisdom and knowledge out of you.

Alzheimer's at the Hippocampus:

Continue Check List for Prayer:

- o Rebuke the spirits of confusion, frustration, agitation, insecurity, forgetfulness, and wanderer
- o Speak healing into the areas of loss memory.
- o Bring strength into your sense of direction.
- o Your purpose is restored into your life.
- o Speak order and a sense of belonging.
- o Speak organization

Amygdala

Physically:

The amygdala is located close to the hippocampus which is in the front portion of the temporal lobe. The amygdala is responsible for the response and memory of the emotions. It is what some researchers have been referring to as the aggression center, and is most commonly known for the emotions of anger, violence, fear, and anxiety.

The most common emotional response produced by the amygdala is fear. It is one of the reasons that we are afraid of things outside of our control. The amygdala is also responsible for the way we react when we are in potentially life threatening and dangerous situations. If the amygdala is overstimulated, it can produce the response of panic and the resulting reactions. The amygdala holds onto these events as memories so that you can relate to it when a similar event takes place.

The amygdala can be the cause of abnormalities in metabolism, blood flow, and different emotions when stimulation occurs. When the amygdala is damaged, then problems like hyperorality, hypersexuality, and disinhibited behavior takes place. Hyperorality is a condition that is characterized by insertion of inappropriate objects in the mouth. Hypersexuality is where someone is exhibiting unusual or excessive concern with or indulgence in sexual activity. Disinhibiting is a lack of restraint manifested in disregard for social conventions, impulsivity, and poor risk assessment.

Other things that can take place when the amygdala is damaged and abnormal functioning has occurred, is things such as anxiety, autism, depression, post-traumatic stress disorder, and phobias. These may also have taken place through developmental problems, damage to the amygdala, and also maybe by an imbalance in the neurotransmitters.

The amygdala is also responsible for depression. This is because the largest emotional response from the amygdala is fear – and the emotional responses that result from that tend to cause a person to withdraw themselves, or to perceive their life as a disaster which might seem 'inescapable'. It is also what brings on social isolation, feeling anxious, and tensed up in unknown situations.

When someone takes medication to regulate their fear and anxiety attacks, or even depression, and they become too mellow; they can lose their ability to be afraid. It can cause them to become foggy in their judgment skills, similar to a person who is under the influence of alcohol. This is why if you or someone you know is taking medication for these types of things to make sure you are keeping an eye on all symptoms that are not considered normal functioning.

Spiritually:

The amygdala is a place where the enemy would have a hay day in lodging more fear, phobias, tormenting spirits of the past, guilt, shame and condemnation just to list a few.

If you are dealing with a spirit of fear you are going to want to remove the roots out of the amygdala and all its emotional ties.

There is a need to understand that there is a good type of fear, and it helps you to survive and have discernment between right and wrong and have the appropriate emotions. But when it becomes overbearing or irrational it needs to be addressed and spirits of fear need to be dislodged. When dealing with the spirit of fear that is not real or unhealthy, and it has formed memories that has connected with the hippocampus, you are going to want to cut them from the hippocampus and remove all triggers that developed with it.

Other spirits you may find that have resided within your amygdala are spirits of isolation, depression, anxiety, rage, anger, murder, violence, irrational fears and things of this nature. On the other end of this you may find spirits of rebellion, disrespect, mockery, pride, arrogance, and things of that nature for those who do not have a healthy fear of God and a respect for the commandments, the law, and for others.

The amygdala is a good place to ask God to help you become balanced in your emotions where you will not overreact in fear but not be a foolish person either. You must be open to hear and receive what God has to say about these areas for they do not work alone. They are affected and also affect other areas in the brain. The Holy Spirit will guide you in the areas that need to be addressed and what is necessary for each individual.

If you come across someone who is continuously worried, full of anxiety, and very fearful, ask God to pour His love into them. The Word of God says that perfect love casts out all fear.

1 John 4:18 (NIV)
"There is no fear in love. But perfect love drives out fear, because fear has to do with punishment. The one who fears is not made perfect in love."

Fear is like a spider web and there is a constant web of different spirits it attaches itself to. Fear roots itself in pain and learned behavior. Address the pain that it feeds off of and ask God to transform the learned behavior and line it up with the Word of God.

Everyone has their own set of triggers of fear and anxiety just like everyone has their own experiences that they go through in life. So each situation and prayer session will reflect these differences. This is why it is so important to be walking in the Spirit of God to be able to address these correctly. It is not a cut and paste situation, and the Word of God also says that we must study to show ourselves approved as well as to be alert and aware of the strategies of the enemy.

2 Timothy 2:15 (NIV)
Do your best to present yourself to God as one approved, a worker who does not need to be ashamed and who correctly handles the word of truth.

2 Corinthians 2:11 (NIV)
in order that Satan should not outwit us. For we are not unaware of his schemes.

If our emotions are not properly managed where they need to be, we may not be able to forgive others – in which case our Heavenly Father will not forgive us. So it is vital to keep our emotions intact and to be able to understand how they come out of balance and how to correctly pray to get them lined back up again. If you are walking in fear, your understanding will become distorted and therefore the ability to forgive can seem to have become quite difficult.

Emotions can be one of the most unexpected responses that you can encounter. A person's emotions can become unstable very quickly. You must be very careful when you are ministering to someone who is not emotionally stable, and ask God if it is a spiritual or physical thing and how He wants it handled. This will bring a security that all will work out and that you will not leave someone unfinished from what God wants to do.

Amygdala – Reflection and Application:

The amygdala is responsible for the response and the memory of emotions. Fear is the most common known response of emotion that the amygdala does.

Damage to the Amygdala may include:

- Abnormalities in metabolism
- Irregularities in blood flow
- Different emotions when stimulated
- Anxiety
- Autism
- Depression
- Post-traumatic stress disorder
- Phobias
- Social isolation

Application Check List:

Spirits to address, rebuke and cast out:

- o Spirit of fear and all its emotional ties.
- o Phobias
- o Tormenting spirits of the past
- o Guilt
- o Shame
- o Condemnation
- o Spirits of isolation
- o Depression
- o Anxiety
- o Rage
- o Anger
- o Murder
- o Violence
- o Irrational fears
- o Spirits of rebellion
- o Disrespect
- o Mockery
- o Pride
- o Arrogance,
- o Ask God to help you become balanced in the emotions.
- o Ask God to pour His love into the emotions. The Word of God says that perfect love casts out all fear.

If you are walking in fear, your understanding will become distorted and the ability to forgive can seem to have become quite difficult.

Hypothalamus

Physically:

The hypothalamus is located under the thalamus. The hypothalamus is responsible for the production of hormones which are known as body messengers. The hormones affect the way your body feels and functions. The hormones control things like the water level in the body, sleep cycles, body temperatures, and food intake.

The hypothalamus produces the hormones that control the production of the hormones within the pituitary gland. There are seven different hormones that the hypothalamus produces:

1. The first hormone is the Anti-Diuretic which regulates water levels in the body, including blood volume and blood pressure. This hormone regulates the amount of water excreted by the kidneys. If you receive too much of the anti-diuretic hormone you can have water retention. If the levels are too low it can cause dehydration or a drop in blood pressure.

2. The second hormone is Oxytocin which is the one that controls some of your behaviors and the reproductive system. High levels of oxytocin have been linked to enlarged prostate glands, while low levels can cause breastfeeding difficulties and symptoms of autism or a lack of social development.

3. The third hormone is the Corticotrophin-Releasing which controls the body's response to physical and emotional stress. It is also responsible for suppressing appetite and stimulating anxiety. If too much of the corticotrophin-releasing hormone is released it can

lead to problems with acne, diabetes, high blood pressure, osteoporosis, infertility and muscle problems. Low levels can cause weight loss, increased skin pigmentation, gastrointestinal distress and low blood pressure.

4. The fourth hormone is the Gonadotropin-Releasing which stimulates the releasing hormones connected to reproductive function, puberty, and sexual maturation. People struggling these hormone levels may notice problems with poor bone health or a lack of fertility. High levels of this hormone can disrupt communication between the hypothalamus and pituitary gland which throws everything off.

5. The fifth hormone is the Samotostatin which inhibits growth and thyroid-stimulating hormones. When this hormone is not functioning correctly it can cause digestive problems, diabetes and gallstones if too much is produced. On the other hand low levels of samotostatin can cause uncontrolled growth hormone secretion, leading to psychological problems.

6. The sixth hormone is the Growth Hormone-Releasing which controls growth and physical development in children as well as metabolism in adults. These hormones, in high levels, can cause abnormal enlargement of the skull, hands and feet, as well as problems with menstruation or diabetes. Low levels can delay puberty in children or decrease muscle mass in adults.

7. The seventh hormone is the Thyrotrophin-Releasing which stimulates production of the thyroid hormone which in turn controls the cardiovascular system, brain development, muscle control, digestive health and metabolism. Finally, patients with high levels of this hormone may experience fatigue, depression, weight gain, constipation, dry skin and hair loss.

Weight loss, weak muscles, excessive sweating and heavy menstrual flow are symptoms of levels that are too low.

Spiritually:

When dealing with the hormones you are going to want to address the hypothalamus. It is the hypothalamus that is producing the hormones. You are going to want to command the communication and the levels to be clear and restored to normal. You are also going to want to remove anything that is blocking or increasing the levels of production.

When your production is off balance you will find yourself open to spirits of lethargy and gluttony among other spirits that would attach itself to any infirmity.

Each hormone that the hypothalamus produces has its own compartment to hide different spirits and sets of problems. Evangelist Barbara Lynch, our pastor, has said multiple times that we are like condominiums inside and each living space needs to be cleansed so that we can be totally clean and receive the fullness that God has for us. This is proof on just how complex the spirit realm can be and how involved it is with our physical bodies.

With the Anti-Diuretic hormone you are going to want to address things such as reducing the level of the hormones to remove all water retention and dry up all trauma water. If the level is too low and you need it to increase you are going to speak hydration and to bring your blood pressure to the correct level. When things like this are present, you need to get before God and ask if there are spirits that are hijacking on these infirmities or symptoms that have manifested themselves.

Another hormone would be oxytocin. It controls some of your behaviors and the reproductive system. There are multiple avenues on what can be going on here and manifesting itself. If you are having issues breastfeeding for instance, you can ask God to regulate and restore your oxytocin hormone to the correct level and function. You can find multiple Scriptures in the Word of God that you can use when addressing these issues as you are finding throughout this book.

As you can see the possibilities can be many, but God is the Creator of you and will know exactly what to tell you. This is where knowing the Holy Spirit and allowing Him to direct and guide you comes into action.

God can and does heal instantaneously but there are times we need to be more in depth and this is just giving you another way of looking at and understanding things and just how complex things can really be.

The Word of God says we pray amiss and most things are because we do not take time to understand and do our part. Or we did not sit in the presence of God long enough to hear all that He has had to say about the situation. More times than not we have found that people will say they are doing these things, but they are not. But your belief in God and in the things that He reveals to you is what brings the lasting results. Many times it is being referred to as walking it out.

Then corticotrophin-releasing is what controls your body's response to stress both physical and emotional. This is one of the reasons why people gain weight and get sick – stress.

When your body is all stressed out it does not function correctly in many areas and becomes weakened. This is a sure open door to a spirit of anxiety, fear and depression, just to name a few. This would be the time to also address what is going on with the amygdala and remove the roots out of the memories of the hippocampus.

You are going to want to apply the scriptures on trusting the Lord and keeping your eyes focused on Him. You are going to want to apply God's peace continuously as you are getting healed and walk in that peace.

The Bible over and over tells you to not live in anxiety and stress but to know He has you and is taking care of it all. The only way this will become real to you is if you apply and meditate on it so that it becomes rooted in your mind and push out the virus of the enemy.

John 14:27 (NIV)
Peace I leave with you; my peace I give you. I do not give to you as the world gives. Do not let your hearts be troubled and do not be afraid.

If you are having a hard time eating, you can pray and ask God to return your appetite to a normal and healthy level and to remove any triggers that would cause you to crave things that would try to bring an artificial comfort to an anxiety that is stimulated.

When symptoms such as diabetes, high blood pressure, low blood pressure, unwanted weight loss, and similar symptoms that come from the corticotrophin-releasing hormone imbalance, you are going to want to go deeper into prayer and address all the parts of the brain that is connected to the symptom that has surfaced. You can do this by researching or reading up on the symptom and being led by the Holy Spirit on what is directly involved with you.

When dealing with the gonadotropin-releasing hormone you are going to want to pray a balance over your children and to remove any triggers, generational curses/spirits/habits, or assignment or anything else the Holy Spirit shows you. If you have a history in your family where you have seen fertility problems or your hypothalamus and pituitary gland is malfunctioning, you are going to want to address this hormone. Ask God to regulate it to the original desire He had for you.

Do not wait for the symptoms to become active. You can address these things as something that is lying dormant and ready to manifest. You are really going to want to do this if you see a timeline pattern in your family line. Even with masturbation, you are going to want to deal with the sexual spirits that is tied to this act and any trauma that comes from the open doors to this.

Now without going off in the wrong direction here and getting off of subject, I want to address very clearly that masturbation is not of God and can be backed up in the Word of God. Whether you want to accept this fact or not, when you are masturbating you are having sex with yourself. This shines the truth on you are committing the sin of fornication and /or adultery if you are practicing such things.

If you have found yourself caught in this sexual web and cannot break the habit, you are going to want to really focus on the areas of your brain that causes the repeated behavior, remove the spirits, and all generational connections so that you can receive your freedom in this area. This is just one of many sins that you have to work at overcoming but understanding where it is entangled in and involved with helps fight it and win.

Addressing the fifth hormone from the physical part of this chapter, the samotostatin, from a spiritual stand point you are going to want to look at the symptoms that leads to issues with your thyroid and your growth. You can also look at it as your growth in the spirit as well.

Let us dig a little deeper. If you are having issues with growing spiritually and it seems that you are stagnating and you are unable to digest the Word like you should or anything in the spiritual realm that you are having (such as similar symptoms) you are going to want to address the spiritual samotostatin. You are going to want to make sure you are removing all spirits that would stop your growth and cause you to have psychological problems.

If you are seeing these symptoms all you have to do is simply command your spiritual samotostatin hormone to become in balance and you can use the Word of God to bring it into balance as you read Scriptures relating to the problems you are facing.

To go along with the samotostatin hormone you are going to want to include the sixth hormone called the growth hormone-releasing hormone. When doing this you are going to want to address the metabolism both in the physical and spiritual sides of this. This is also where you are going to want to focus on asking God to heal if and when you see symptoms of this hormone not working, such as, but not limited to, delay in puberty, decrease in muscle mass, and problems with different body parts not being the correct size – such as an oversized skull.

When you see these symptoms ask God to send down His Holy Healing Ointment- His Balm Of Gilead. When these parts are being healed, pray the Balm of Gilead to run down to the root of the problem so that it has to line up to the way God has made you or the person you are praying for.

Tagging along with dealing with the fifth and sixth hormone you are also going to want to address the thyrotrophin-releasing hormone. You are going to want to address this hormone when addressing the thyroid and any malfunctions that may be found or symptoms that may manifest themselves.

Pray against any illegitimate control over the cardiovascular system, brain development as well as muscle control, digestive health and metabolism. Rebuke and cast out all controlling spirits that would be operating to make your hormones too high or too low.

You can command your weight to be at the correct weight in the mighty name of Jesus. You can command all fatigue and depression and all spirits associated to be removed and cast down to the pit of hell.

You do not have to accept the enemy in these areas. Use the Word of God against the enemy. If you are suffering from depression, look up depression in the Word. When you find it, speak the Words of life over yourself and watch what the amazing Words of God can do for you and how it can transform your physical and spiritual mind.

Hypothalamus – Reflection and Application:

The hypothalamus is responsible for the producing of hormones - body messengers. The hormones control things like the water level in the body, sleep cycles, body temperatures, and food intake.

1. Anti-Diuretic
2. Oxytocin
3. Corticotrophin-Releasing
4. Gonadotropin-Releasing
5. Somatostatin
6. Growth Hormone-Releasing
7. Thyrotropin-releasing

Application check list on individual hormones:

Anti-Diuretic hormone
- o Remove all water retention
- o Dry up all trauma water
- o If levels too low – increase and bring adequate hydration
- o Ask God to make blood pressure to the correct level.

Oxytocin
If issues breastfeeding – ask God to regulate and restore the oxytocin to the correct level and function.

Corticotrophin-releasing
Stress:
Corticotrophin-releasing hormones control your body's response to stress, both physical and emotional. Stress is one of the major reasons why people gain weight and get sick.

- Remove the stress
- Close the "open door" to the spirit of anxiety, fear and depression

Overeating:
If you are having a difficult time with overeating:

- Command your appetite to return to a normal and healthy level
- Remove any triggers
- Remove the craving of things that would bring an artificial comfort to anxiety that has been stimulated.

Hormone Imbalance Symptoms:

- Diabetes
- High blood pressure
- Low blood pressure
- Unwanted weight loss

Gonadotropin-releasing
Check your family history for fertility problems, hypothalamus and pituitary gland malfunctioning.

List generational curses/spirits/habits, or assignments in the history in your family. Look for any timeline patterns in your family history, including sexual habits.

- o Break the generational curses
- o Rebuke and cast out the generational spirits, fragments, soul invaders, and heart parts
- o Break the ungodly and destructive assignments over your family
- o Speak hormone balance over your children.
- o Remove any triggers
- o Rebuke and cast out all sexual spirits
- o Destroy the sexual web.
- o Destroy repeated behavior
- o Remove the spirits that has cause the repeated behavior
- o Remove all generational connections

Somatostatin
Somatostatin inhabits growth and your thyroid stimulation. Have you been having issues with growing spiritually and it seems that you are stagnating and you are unable to digest the Word?

Address:
- o Removing all spirits stop your growth
- o Address any psychological problems.
- o Command your "spiritual somatostatin" hormone to become in balance.
- o Dig into the Word of God and read Scriptures relating to the problems you are having and claim the Scriptures over yourself.

Growth hormone-releasing
Address the metabolism, delay in puberty, and decrease in muscle mass, problems with different body parts not being the correct size – such as an oversized skull. Apply the Holy

Healing Ointment – the Balm of Gilead upon these areas and speak life.

Thyrotrophin-releasing hormone
Address the thyroid in prayer and list any malfunctions and symptoms that you are having coming from the thyroid not functioning properly.

Pray against any illegitimate control over:
- o Cardiovascular system
- o Brain development
- o Muscle control
- o Digestive health
- o Metabolism

Address the following:
- o Remove all controlling spirits
- o Command your weight to be at the correct weight
- o Command all fatigue and depression and all spirits associated to be removed and cast down to the pit of hell
- o Remove the spirits of lethargy and gluttony
- o Remove the infirmity that had attached itself to any of the spirits that had been removed.

Hormones

Physically & Spiritually:

Sin can cause these hormones to come out of balance. For instance, if you are into pornography and dopamine is released in this way to cause you to want sex or sexual intimacy then your body will release the hormones of oxytocin. The oxytocin will bond you to the pornographic images, actors or actresses and sexual acts. This can really throw your sexual behavior out of whack as well as your reproductive system. All sin brings a consequence and sexual sins can bring on some of the priciest ones.

1 Corinthians 6:18-20 (NIV)
18 Flee from sexual immorality. All other sins a person commits are outside the body, but whoever sins sexually, sins against their own body.
19 Do you not know that your bodies are temples of the Holy Spirit, who is in you, whom you have received from God? You are not your own;
20 you were bought at a price. Therefore honor God with your bodies.

When something like this takes place it does not just affect one area but many areas. I have personally experienced watching and helping people with sexual issues being out of sorts by sin and bad habits. I watch them struggle with self-hatred, anger, discontent, pride, selfishness, depression, gluttony and manipulation, just to name a few.

Things like this can really run a person's life and that is why the enemy is fighting so hard to mess these things up. But the truth is it is up to us to make the decision to yield and let God help us overcome these changes and walk in a new life that He has designed.

We have seen case after case where men in particular have problems with erectile dysfunction as well as an imbalanced appetite that causes issues in their marriage or to their self-esteem. Other effects of too much oxytocin can result in enlarged prostate glands. If you are receiving too low it can cause breastfeeding problems and symptoms of autism or a lack of social development.

One of the biggest reasons people are overweight is because your hormones are out of balance. It would be one of the most effective places for a spirit of gluttony to be hidden. Shine the Light of Christ on the spirit and remove it. Shine the light of God into your hormones and remove every spirit and get the levels back to the way they are to be. But there is a part for us to do in this process also and that is to take care of ourselves spiritually, physically and emotionally.

Hormonal imbalances also trigger a range of other symptoms such as PMS, acne, migraines, cellulite, loss of libido, a disrupted monthly cycle, menopausal issues and burn-outs. So recognizing these triggers you can trace back to the hormones and address it. Ask the Holy Spirit to reveal the truth on what is going on and how to fix it. But in the process you are going to have to remove the spirits and deal with the emotional issues associated with it as well.

Just about every problem you face in your body is trauma related in one way or another. So you need to make sure you drain the pain and emotions and restore your hormones back into the correct functional level that God has created you to have it at.

Realizing that your hormones dictate virtually every part of your life is a big revelation that can change the way you view things and how you are praying. It can change things from your state of mind to your behavior, body shape, eating habits and even your reaction to stress. Where all these things are affected there are many spirits and things going on in the spirit realm that are lodging and hiding. They want to stay so they can torment you and pull you out of your destiny with God.

As you address the spirits, fragments, invaders, heart parts, emotions, pain, triggers, devices, and anything else that are attached, you will see that you can walk so much closer to God. You are capable of doing this because you are lining up your body as the temple of God and making the necessary changes.

In the following Chapter we will discuss the glands within the brain.

Hormones – Reflection and Application:

Sin can cause hormones to become out of balance. For instance, every time you involve yourself into the addiction of pornography, dopamine is released and then you develop an ungodly and unhealthy desire to want sex or sexual intimacy. The release of the hormones oxytocin, if it is in an ungodly manner, will throw your sexual behavior out of whack as well as your reproductive system. All sin brings a consequence and sexual sins can bring on some of the priciest ones.

Sin and bad habits open the doors to spirits such as: self-hatred, anger, discontentment, pride, selfishness, depression, gluttony, manipulation, etc.

If you continue in the sexual sin you can develop problems such as erectile dysfunction, an imbalanced sexual appetite or an enlarged prostate gland.

Imbalanced hormones can also cause breastfeeding problems, symptoms of autism, a lack of social development or being overweight.

Hormonal imbalances also trigger a range of other symptoms such as PMS, acne, migraines, cellulite, loss of libido, a disrupted monthly cycle, menopausal issues and emotional burn-outs.

If you find that you have a hormone imbalance, you need to really search yourself and your family line to see if sin is the cause for the imbalance.

- List the sins that you and/or your family lines have committed that caused the imbalance of the hormones.

- Ask God to forgive you and your ancestors for the sins. The more specific you are the better.

- Ask God to drain the pain and emotion attached to the sin and imbalanced hormones.

- Directly address what the problem is and command it to return to normal.

- Ask God to restore your hormones back into the correct functional level that God has created you to have.

- List the Spirits that God revealed are attached to the sin or generational curse that was there and rebuke and cast them out. There could be spirits such as:

- Self-hatred
- Anger
- Discontentment
- Pride
- Selfishness
- Depression
- Gluttony
- Manipulation

Speak healing and restoration in the areas addressed and complete balance to the hormones.

Pituitary Gland:

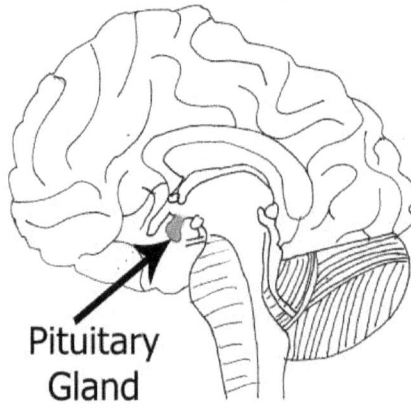

Pituitary Gland

Physically:

The pituitary gland controls growth, body temperature, pregnancy and childbirth. It is located at the base of the brain. The pituitary gland controls the function of most other endocrine glands, this is why it is at times called the master gland. Between the hypothalamus and the pituitary gland, depending on the level of hormones levels that are produced, it can determine how much stimulations the target glands need.

Here is a chart on the hormones and that target organ or tissue:

Hormone	Target Organ or Tissue
Adrenocorticotropic hormone (ACTH)	Adrenal glands
Beta-melanocyte–stimulating hormone	Skin
Endorphins	Brain and immune system
Enkephalins	Brain
Follicle-stimulating hormone	Ovaries or testes
Growth hormone	Muscles and bones
Luteinizing hormone	Ovaries or testes
Oxytocin	Uterus and mammary glands
Prolactin	Mammary glands
Thyroid-stimulating hormone	Thyroid gland
Vasopressin (antidiuretic hormone)	Kidneys

The pituitary has two distinct parts: Front lobe (anterior) and Rear lobe (posterior).

The hypothalamus controls the front lobe by releasing hormones through the connecting blood vessels. It controls the rear lobe through nerve impulses.

It is the front lobe of the pituitary that produces and releases these main hormones: Growth hormone, Thyroid-stimulating hormone, Corticotrophin, Gonadotropins, Prolactin. You can see the description and more details of these things in the chapter earlier under the hypothalamus.

The rear lobe of the pituitary produces only two hormones: Vasopressin and Oxytocin.

The pituitary gland can malfunction in several ways, usually as a result of developing a noncancerous tumor. Too little or too much of a pituitary hormone can result in a wide variety of symptoms. Some disorders that result from overproduction of pituitary hormones include erectile dysfunction, prolactin, and growth hormone. Other disorders that result from underproduction of pituitary hormones include hypopituitarism which is multiple hormones not functioning correctly and central diabetes.

Spiritually:

Spiritually you would want to focus on this area when you are praying for someone who is or is trying to get pregnant. You can also pray health to this area for someone who has diabetes, tumors (cancerous or non-cancerous), has sexual problems and different disorders that can be affected by sin or generational iniquity that has been passed down the generations.

By that I mean, if you have been in perversion and have suffered from an erectile dysfunction then you are going to want to repent for your sin. When that is completed then command the pituitary gland to be normalized in function and speak health to it.

If your ancestors have been into perversion then you are going to want to repent on their behalf and then speak regulation and health to the gland. This is only one of many things that you would be able to pray for in the spirit realm. Each case may be different, but you should be really seeking God's face and see what He has to say about it. After all He is the one who created you, knows your makeup and design, and what will work for you.

Pituitary Gland – Reflection and Application:

The pituitary gland controls growth, body temperature, pregnancy and childbirth. The pituitary gland controls the function of most other endocrine glands. The front lobe of the pituitary produces: Growth hormone, Thyroid-stimulating hormone, Corticotrophin, Gonadotropins and Prolactin. The back lobe of the pituitary produces only two hormones: Vasopressin and Oxytocin.

Some disorders that result from overproduction of pituitary hormones include erectile dysfunction, prolactin and growth hormone. Underproduction of pituitary hormones includes hypopituitarism and diabetes.

Prayer Check List:

You are going to want to include the pituitary gland in with the prayers that you pray for each hormone listed above.

Other times you are going to want to pray for the pituitary gland and address it for those who are, or is, trying to get pregnant for health and balance and during their pregnancy clear up to the child birthing process, someone who has diabetes, tumors, has sexual problems, and sexual sins that have effected them due to sin or generational sins that have been passed down.

If captivity in perversion is a factor and they have suffered from an erectile dysfunction then you are going to have to repent for the sin. If your ancestors have been into perversion then you are going to want to repent on their behalf and then speak regulation and health to the gland. (Revisit the hormone check list).

Pineal Gland

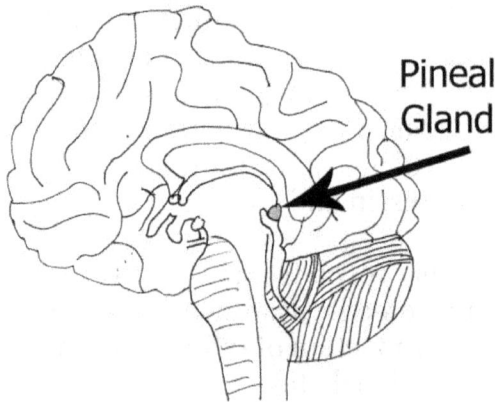

Pineal Gland

Physically:

The pineal gland is known as the "tiny gland". It has also been called the third eye. It controls sleep, circadian rhythms, and the natural internal clock. It actually has retina tissue and made up of photoreceptors just like an eyeball. The main function of the pineal gland is to produce melatonin. Melatonin is secreted by the pineal gland enters the bloodstream, where it flows to its target cells throughout the body. It is what helps modulate sleep patterns. In the brain, it causes a sense of drowsiness that is associated with nighttime.

Circadian rhythms are important in determining the sleeping and feeding patterns of all animals and human beings. Circadian rhythm is roughly a 24 hour cycle in the physiological process of living beings. There are clear patterns of brain activity, hormone production, cell regeneration, and other biological activities linked to this daily cycle.

Food For Thought:

If your sleep is all off balance, could it be that there is a spirit that has caused the timing to be off and is using it as a way to torment you and make you weak and unable to fight properly?

Spiritually:

You can look at this two or more different ways. One way is to recognize this as an attack originating from the spirit realm that is manifesting the side effects in your physical body. The other way to look at this is to recognize this as an attack against your effectiveness in serving God.

With the first way, you are going to want to ask God to regulate your melatonin if you are having an issue relaxing and sleeping. You may have a baby who has their days and nights mixed up, and one way you can pray for this is to pray for the regulation of the release of melatonin and the regulation of the sleep cycle and rhythm.

When your rhythm is off it would make sense that you would not be able to function or think when your body is trying to tell you that you are tired and you ignore it. You find yourself pushing your limits to stay up or using artificial things to keep you awake. This will cause an issue of imbalance and timing that is not synchronized. It can and will result in a consequence of your sleep and energy being off and not being able to be as productive as you should be if you were getting plenty of both.

You would need to repent for doing something outside of God's strength and pressing your body's ability to go further than it should in your own strength. Then ask God to help you with the consequences and speak health and normalization to these areas and get you back on track. There are reasons why God says to rest in Him. He wants us to be strengthened so that we can face whatever comes our way. He is the only one who knows what tomorrow holds.

Spiritually you may feel lethargic and use worldly motivations as the way to do anything that God has asked you to do, instead of it coming as second nature from the teachings and lessons you receive from the Holy Spirit.

Pineal Gland - Reflection and Application:

The pineal gland is known as the third eye. It controls sleep, circadian rhythms and the natural internal clock. It produce melatonin. Melatonin enters the bloodstream, helps modulate sleep patterns, and gives a sense of drowsiness that is associated with nighttime.

Ask God to regulate your melatonin if you are having an issue to relax and sleep. Pray for the regulation of the release of melatonin and the regulation of the sleep cycle and rhythm if they are off track.

Spiritually you may feel lethargic and use worldly motivations as the way to be able to do anything that God has asked you to do instead of it coming as second nature and the teachings that you have been given to become a part of life.

List the things that you feel you are lethargic with:

- o Take authority over all spirits of laziness and lethargy and command them to be cast out. Speak renewal and proper balance into your health, energy and body – to line up according to the Word of God.
- o Line up your body under your soul.
- o Command your soul to receive healing.
- o Line up your soul under your spirit.
- o Command your spirit to be made whole and healed.
- o Line up your spirit under the Holy Spirit and the Holy Spirit will continue to fill and protect you as the work is being finished.

Conclusion

In this world so many spiritual practices and religions have found many benefits to the importance of being mentally healthy and just how it does affect your life.

The world is looking for something to believe in that will bring meaning to their life and to relieve them of suffering that they have gone through. They want to recover from the trauma and pain that they have had to endure.

As they pursue looking to another source, their faith in it brings a better health outcome, but not necessarily a completed one if they are not believing in the one and only true God. They may find temporary fixes such as greater longevity, coping skills and health-related quality of life with less anxiety, depression and suicide. But to receive the ultimate and completed healing it has to come from God Himself.

There is so much to be learned about life and about God and how He created us. And to imagine we have not even scratched the surface of what God has revealed to His people. Even with what we know up to this point we have a hard time keeping up with it and living it out.

Now that you have an idea on how the brain works and understanding how the enemy will try to use it against you, that you have more wisdom how to fight him and get rid of the demon spirits that he hides inside of us to try to separate us from God.

We must see that a Christian life is not all about sunshine and roses. It is about sacrificing through our love for the Father to bring others into His Kingdom just as He has done for us. For us to do this we must apply what we learn to become more like Christ so that we can give out the unconditional love as He does. This is what the world does not know but needs so desperately.

As you dive in deeper into your prayer life and into ministering to others you will be able to utilize what you have learned. I believe that this will only be the beginning of more knowledge and wisdom to come as God downloads more to you.

You do not have to accept a disease, a bad habit, a bad behavior pattern, nor do you have to accept sin. Jesus Christ died on the Cross for you and I so that we were not bound to the slavery of such things.

As you see that different parts of the brains activity affects your daily life, you can speak health into it, completely full function, and anything else God will reveal to you. But the things you have learnt so far will get you going in the right direction. You do not have to accept being sick. It is God's desire that His children be well and of a sound mind.

We have found as we do the work of the Father that the Word of God does transform your brain. It restores and brings health into damaged brain cells as well as increases brain activity. The Word of God tells you that the Word brings life and not death but the key is to apply it to your life.

You can read the Word of God and it will not do anything for you until you start believing the Word. When you read the Word into your life and allow your belief system to engage with it, that is when the real change takes place.

As you apply what you learn from the Word of God to your life you will find that your soul is being healed, your brain will become healed, your body will function correctly and then you will watch prosperity take place. I am not just talking about prosperity in finances but health, spiritually, and on all areas of your life.

There are so many reasons why the Word of God mentions about your mind and that you have to do your part in keeping under the subjection of God and crucify any and all vain imaginations that rise up against God.

If you are not doing your part, it is the same as seeing that you have a bleeding wound from an artery and not doing anything about it. In this instance you will die. You will also spiritually die if you do not get your brain lined up to God and evict the demons who hide and hijack different parts of your mind.

The choice really is up to you and if you are praying for someone else it would be a good idea for you to ask God for the strategy and battle plan. This will help you know how far you are committing into what is laid before you.

Assignments can be a prayer, a month of ministry, or until completion. But when dealing with someone's mind it is a very delicate thing and must be done in the Spirit through the leading of the Holy Spirit.

The Word of God says some of us plant the seed, some water it and others harvest it. But you have to ask God what is your part in each person's life because it can change. It can change simply because of a decision the person makes.

Stay in tune with God and seek Him continuously. When you do this, your relationship with God will go from one level to the next, to the next. It will go higher and higher. Change after change will take place and God's Glory will be manifested in your life continuously.